ISRAEL
AND THE PALESTINIAN NIGHTMARE

Ze'ev Shemer

ISRAEL AND THE PALESTINIAN NIGHTMARE

"I do not recognize your authority to try me" is Dov Gruner's last statement on April 19, 1947 before being dragged to the gallows by the British Authorities.

This court has no legal foundation, since it is appointed by a regime without legal foundation. You came to Palestine because of the commitment you undertook at the behest of all the nations of the world to rectify the greatest wrong caused to any nation in the history of mankind, namely the expulsion of Israel from their land, which transformed them into victims of persecution and incessant slaughter throughout the world. It is this commitment - and this commitment alone - which constituted the legal and moral basis for your presence in this country. But you betrayed it willfully, brutally and with satanic cunning. You turned your commitment into a mere scrap of paper...

When the prevailing government in any country is not legal, when it becomes a regime of oppression and tyranny, it is the right of its citizens - more than that, it is their duty - to fight this regime and to topple it. This is what Jewish youth are doing and will continue to do until you quit this land, and hand it over to its rightful owners: the Jewish people. For you should know this: there is no power in the world which can sever the tie between the Jewish people and their one and only land. Whosoever tries to sever it – his hand will be cut off and the curse of God will rest on him forever."

Dov Gruner HY"D

On April 19, 1947, the British Mandatory Authorities in Palestine sentenced Dov Gruner to death. He is executed for his role in the pre-state Jewish underground.

HaShem Yimkom Damo.

TABLE OF CONTENTS

"The truth is incontrovertible,

malice may attack it,

ignorance may deride it,

but in the end;

there it is."

Winston Churchill

PREFACE

What is the Arab-Israeli conflict? Most people would assume it has to do with the struggle of the Palestinian people. This however, may not explain the violent unrests that occurred before the world heard of a people called Palestinian. Then maybe it has to do with the occupation of lands taken during the 1967 war; lands referred to as the West Bank. But that does not explain the two wars that occurred prior to that event. Yet, it is the images of Palestinian children being "oppressed" by Israeli soldiers that represent the most clear mental picture for the words 'Arab-Israeli conflict'. So maybe it has to do with Jewish people, mainly Jews from Russia and Eastern Europe, who arrived in the land of Palestine shortly after WWII and took over a land that did not belong to them. Today Israelis, mostly sons and daughters of these immigrants, are currently 'occupying' the land of the Palestinian people. The world has seen thousands of reports of abuse and violence against these 'native' Arabs who have been stripped from their homes and their land, and are subjected to daily hardship and humiliation, results of this unfair occupation.

This sounds like a logical explanation, right? Wrong. Not even close.

There isn't a single Israeli politician that does not support the unsound proposal of two-states for two peoples. There isn't a single leader that does not offer unilateral concessions in order to appease the world powers and attempt to reach some kind of agreement with an entity that has not and will never recognize its right to exist. To them, Israel is 'Palestine,' and the Arab world will continue its struggle against the "Zionist" occupation of a land they claim is "theirs". Jews will continue to timidly defend themselves under the watchful eye of world powers who more than ever support the plight of the Palestinian people. A nuclear Iran, the downfall of America, the collapse of Europe can all become cataclysmic factors that can seal the fate of a people who are too weak and too frightened to lay claim to what is rightfully theirs.

"When all is said and done and all the causes are separated from the effects, it becomes clear that the ultimate sin of the people who rule the State of Israel is that they have done everything to remove the significance, the magnificence and the sweetness of victory from the great miracle of Return and resurrection of the Jewish state.

What they have done and do daily is to turn the miraculous into the ordinary, the hallowed into the profane and the truth of the matter is that, because of this all the miracles and wonders that have occurred to us in the nature of rebirth of the Land have come about, not so much because of the ruling circles, but despite them.

People that have been the most debased of losers for 2,000 years find it difficult to cope with victory. It finds it extraordinary difficult to remain normal. It inherits insecurities, complexes, guilt. It begins to believe its enemies' slanders. It loses its self-respect and longs for the love of a hating world. There is nothing ethical about dying or anything moral about another holocaust. There is nothing immoral about winning and nothing necessarily noble in a loser. Let us cast off the chains of guilt and reject the accusations of its bearers. The greatness of Judaism is its spirit, but no spirit can survive without a living body."

Before you complete the reading of this book, you will be able to put a name to the quote above. You will also be able to answer to those that accuse you of usurpation. You will understand what Zionism is, what Palestine really means, and why you will never be allowed to speak the truth with ease of mind and spirit, and without putting your life in mortal danger.

Your quest for the truth, begins now.

> "In every generation, there are always a few who understand;
> Always understand... even if you remain among the few."
> RABBI MEIR KAHANE

INTRODUCTION

Five hundred million Arabs; five million Jews.
Think of all the Arab countries as a football field,
and Israel as a pack of matches sitting in the middle of it.
Larry Miller

As of 2013 the population of the Middle East is composed of 6 million Jews who live in Israel and 366 million Arabs (mostly Muslim) who live in the surrounding countries including 2 million within Israel's borders. There are 56 countries that have a Muslim majority, dozens that have a Christian majority and even four nations that have a Hindu majority; there is however, only one country where there is a Jewish majority and although Israel is no larger than the Sate of New Jersey, it seems that one country is apparently one country too many for the world to bear. This rejection of a Jewish state is the at the center of the most intensely monitored conflict in the world. Many believe that this volatility could spark the next world war.

Volatility however, is more of a serious and common phenomenon among the Muslim nations that surround Israel, rather than in Israel itself.

The Center for Systemic Peace published in its 2011 Global Report a detailed assessment of "state fragility" for each of the world's 165 major countries with populations greater than 500,000. Their rating system accounts for effectiveness and legitimacy indicators for security, governance, economic, and social dimensions of state performance.

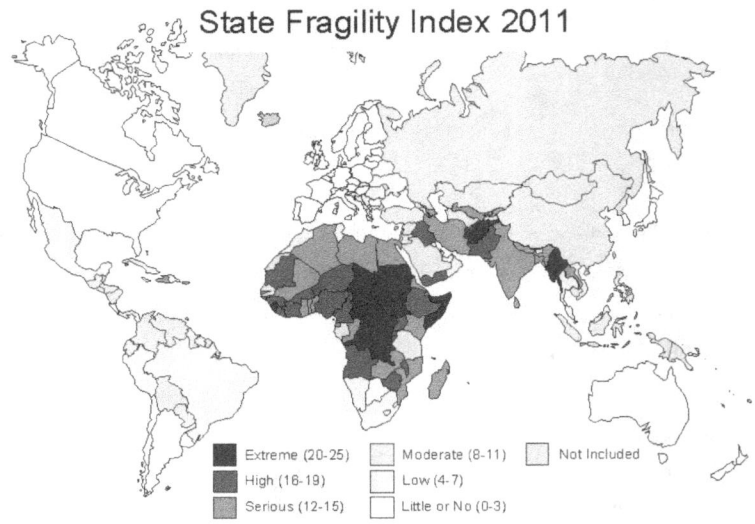

State Fragility Index 2011

Extreme (20-25)   Moderate (8-11)   Not Included
High (16-19)   Low (4-7)
Serious (12-15)   Little or No (0-3)

It is very difficult to ignore that all countries marked as Extreme, High and Serious are Islamic nations with the exceptions of India, where Muslims account for 14% of their population and Israel, where Muslims account for 17% of their population. Half of the world's countries labeled as having a Moderate state of fragility are Muslim nations, while 20% of the remaining countries in this category have significant Islamic populations as well.

Volatility is just one factor that sets the Islamic world apart. Their constant state of conflict and readiness to adopt armed struggle in order to further their political and religious goals has wound up the world to a state of tension not experienced since the rise of the Third Reich. More than half of the current conflicts around the world today involve Islamic factions. Whether it is the violent conflict of Muslims versus Slavs in Bosnia, Albania, Kosovo; or Muslims versus secularists and Christians in countries such as Armenia, Azerbaijan, Cyprus, Algeria, Sudan, Egypt, Eritrea, Ethiopia.

Moreover, there's the ongoing war in Iraq and Afghanistan were many times Muslims have attacked Kurds and Christians in addition to allied forces. In other countries were non-Christians are practically non-existent, there is ongoing violence between Muslim sects (e.g., Sunnis, Shiites, and Alawites).

In Asia Muslim groups have targeted Christians, Hindus and Jews; and have also been known to attack secularists even if they are Muslims themselves (e.g., Pakistan, India, China, Chechnya, Philippines, Indonesia and Uzbekistan).

Undoubtedly, the most intensely scrutinized conflict today, is the one involving Israel. Internally Muslim sects are constantly at odds with each other and heinous acts of violence are reported when Hamas and Fatah leaders compete for power. Inside of Israel proper, Christians are persecuted and often harassed by Muslims in cities that for years were known to be mostly Christian such as Bethlehem and Nazareth. Of course, it is the hatred of the Jews and the Jewish state that generates the most widespread violence. However, as you read this book you will understand that those that spouse hatred and violence are only a fraction of the total population, lead by a vocal and powerful minority, that if we were to remove them from power, the consequence would probably be a joint effort for mutual prosperity. This, however, has proven to be an unrealistic goal.

The biggest threat to world stability today is Iran and their desperate race to complete their military nuclear program. The outgoing president of the Islamic republic, Mahmoud Ahmadinejad, vouched to "wipe Israel off the map", something his colleague and new Iranian leader Hassan Rohani supports wholeheartedly. This does not answer the question of what exactly is the Arab-Israeli conflict? What is it about? Who is to blame? And how will it ever be resolved? These are basic questions that touch upon the most important political arena the world has known since the end of the Second World War. There must be a reason that the 'atrocities' that are occurring or are alleged to be occurring in Israel are not overshadowed by the myriads of killings of innocents in Syria, Somalia, Rwanda, Sudan, Egypt, Afghanistan, Yemen and Iraq among others. What makes this particular conflict so exceptional?

Unlike other conflicts, and contrary to popular belief, the Arab-Israeli conflict is not about land, occupation, political discord, or a dispute over the historical legitimacy and ownership of a tiny corner of real estate in the Middle East. Especially a land that historically was best described as a sea of sand and rocks, and until recently had no known natural resources[1]. This particular conflict is rooted in a much more comprehensive issue. Israel today is at the front line of a war between the civilized world and an Islamic all-encompassing system of life that is at odds with the values of Western civilization. It is a battle between Islam and the rest of the world; between Ishmael and Isaac and everything they represent. A battle between Islamists stuck in time, caught up in a web of violence and fanaticism, and Jews, leading the world in cutting-edge technology and development while preserving their unbreakable bond to ancient yet universally accepted standards of morality.

Judaism and Islam both repudiate idolatry, yet one invalidates the other. Land is a pretext. Occupation, refugee camps, displaced masses, it is all but an elaborate smoke screen. Without trivializing the suffering of those caught in this evil web, the truth is, land is the least of the underlying factors that fuels this unending war; it is however, the best excuse and the preferred tool to exert pressure and foment hatred against the Jewish people. This hatred is hardly new. It dates much farther back than 1948 when the Jewish State was reborn. The hatred of the Jews is the hatred of the messenger and the rejection of the message.

Arabs who reside within Israel claim they have nowhere else to go, and Jews cannot bear to throw them out. Violence breaks out and the conflict continues. And this conflict undoubtedly is the most intensely watched, scrutinized, involved and complex battle scene on planet earth.

The question is, how did this conflict come about? And why are there any doubts about the legitimate ownership of the land of Israel? There are several answers to this thorny question; but ultimately it boils down to accepting one of two main

---

[1] Recent discoveries of enormous natural gas reserves were found off the coast of Haifa within the last five years.

points of view, either the Jewish point of view or the Muslim assertion of reality. It is imperative to understand however, that not every Jew subscribes to the Jewish point of view, and not every Muslim agrees with the Islamic take on the issues. And then, there's the rest of humanity, some split between the two, but with an overwhelming majority abstaining from issuing an educated opinion. After all, who are we kidding? We live in an ever increasingly impervious, egotistic and parsimonious world.

Israel's conflict with its Muslim counterpart is only secondary to its internal fiery affairs. It is my contention that Israel's worst enemies, those who hurt her the most, are by far the 'unJews' - Jews by birth who suffer from self-loathing and are known for their perceived need to bend over backwards seeking incessantly for the world's approval. They express loudly and sometimes violently their contempt against Israel and its inherent Jewish identity. The reason for this pathological behavior is complex. Their behavior seems to be driven by self-hatred and possibly has more to do with their rejection of God and traditional Judaism than their 'passionate quest for justice' and the unconditional support of the Palestinian cause.

It is important to note that not all Arabs agree with the Muslim assertion that Israel has no right to exist. Many Arabs are Christians, and most certainly do not accept the Islamists' point of view. Many of the people incorrectly branded as Arabs, are actually Druze and Kurds, and most would also disagree with the anti-Israel stand held by the majority of the Muslim populace of the world. Furthermore, some Israeli-Arabs, even Muslims by faith, see themselves as regular Israeli citizens, and do not identify with the Palestinian people or their contentions.

To better understand what the Arab-Israeli conflict is all about we need to define the terms, define the players and look at the Middle East having a clear historical viewpoint. Watching CNN or the BBC will certainly not provide any intelligent human being with an objective picture of the real issues that have been inflaming this seemingly endless conflict. Mainstream media is today synonymous of political propaganda and is subject to continuous manipulation.

What most people think to know about the Arab-Israeli conflict can be surmised as I stated in the preface of this book: The Jewish people, mainly Jews from Russia and Eastern Europe, arrived in the land of Palestine shortly after WWII and took over a land that did not belong to them. Today Israelis, mostly sons and daughters of these immigrants, are currently 'occupying' the land of the Palestinian people. Nothing can be farther from the truth.

The reality is far more complicated than what we are being told on a regular basis by the world media, the political manipulators, and the majority of the world's academic and pseudo-academic circles. Joseph Goebles[2] once said "If you tell a lie big enough and keep repeating it, people will eventually come to believe it." Goebles' motivation was his deep-seated hatred of the Jewish people, and there is a chilling relation between today's accusers and those who mastered the art of propaganda and mass brainwashing. To acquire a clear understanding we must look at historical data, while keeping in mind, that new facts were also created as a result of wars, expulsions, population transfers, mass deportations, and responses to violence and terrorism.

For centuries, the land of Israel (Palestine) was mostly barren land temporarily occupied or ruled by an assortment of foreign empires that ruled over a very small number of people. Many came and left, and not once did any establish a country, a permanent stronghold, or a viable state. The Bedouin Arabs, the Jews and the small number of Christians that made Israel their home, were poor, desolate and most survived thanks to foreign charitable contributions, mainly from Jews in the diaspora. Massive expulsions of Jews, and the genocide known as the Holocaust, caused a considerable number of refugees to come to Israel and build a country in the desert and swamplands, in the land the Romans once renamed Palestine.

---

[2] Joseph Goebbels was a German politician and Reich Minister of Propaganda in Nazi Germany from 1933 to 1945.

Shortly before the State of Israel was reborn in 1948, people referred to as Palestinian were Jews, Christians and Arabs that lived in what today constitutes Israel, Jordan and the Palestinian territories, and were unwillingly ruled by the British. Prior to that, residents of this barren land lived under the rule of the Ottoman Empire (Turkey) and prior to that, Palestine is a term that represented this same desolate land where the Biblical kingdoms of Israel and Judea once existed.

There is a writer that uses the pen name of Yashiko Sagamori. She wrote a piece back in 2002 that created quite a stir in the academic world. She asked a series of questions that were seemingly impossible to answer as her response to a pseudo-academic that ranted in favor of the Palestinian cause. Here is Sagamori in her own words:

"If you are so sure that Palestine the country, goes back through most of recorded history, I expect you to be able to answer a few basic questions about that country of Palestine:

When is it founded and by whom? What were its borders? What is its capital? What were its major cities? What constituted the basis of its economy? What is its form of government? Can you name at least one Palestinian leader before Arafat? Is Palestine ever recognized by a country whose existence, at that time or now, leaves no room for interpretation?

What is the language of the country of Palestine? What is the prevalent religion of the country of Palestine? What is the name of its currency? Choose any date in history and tell what is the approximate exchange rate of the Palestinian monetary unit against the US dollar, German mark, GB pound, Japanese yen, or Chinese yuan on that date.

And, finally, since there is no such country today, what caused its demise and when did it occur?

You are lamenting the "low sinking" of a "once proud" nation. Please tell me, when exactly is that "nation" proud and what is it so proud of?

And here is the least sarcastic question of all: If the people you mistakenly call 'Palestinians" are anything but generic Arabs collected from all over -- or thrown out of -- the Arab world, if they really have a genuine ethnic identity that gives them right for self-determination, why did they never try to become independent until Arabs suffered their devastating defeat in the Six Day War (1967)?

I hope you avoid the temptation to trace the modern day "Palestinians" to the Biblical Philistines: substituting etymology for history won't work here. The truth should be obvious to everyone who wants to know it. Arab countries have never abandoned the dream of destroying Israel; they still cherish it today. Having time and again failed to achieve their evil goal with military means, they decided to fight Israel by proxy. For that purpose, they created a terrorist organization, cynically called it "the Palestinian people" and installed it in Gaza, Judea, and Samaria. How else can you explain the refusal by Jordan and Egypt to unconditionally accept back the 'West Bank' and Gaza, respectively?

The fact is, Arabs populating Gaza, Judea, and Samaria have much less claim to nationhood than that Indian tribe that successfully emerged in Connecticut with the purpose of starting a tax-exempt casino: at least that tribe had a constructive goal that motivated them. The so-called 'Palestinians' have only one motivation: the destruction of Israel, and in my book that is not sufficient to consider them a nation - or anything else except what they really are: a terrorist organization that will one day be dismantled. In fact, there is only one way to achieve peace in the Middle East. Arab countries must acknowledge and accept their defeat in their war against Israel and, as the losing side should, pay Israel reparations for the more than 50 years of devastation they have visited on it. The most appropriate form of such reparations would be the removal of their terrorist organization from the land of Israel and accepting Israel's ancient sovereignty over Gaza,

Judea, and Samaria. That will mark the end of the Palestinian people. What are you saying again is its beginning?"

In this book I will attempt to explain Sagamori's position and hopefully answer some of the questions she poses above. However, in order to understand the issues at hand we'll have to look at the history of the creation of Israel, the current disputes, the internal struggle, the war between Jews and unJews[3], the dilemmas of the Arab people, the desires and goals of our Arab neighbors, and the political and religious consequences of accepting a Jewish State in the middle of the Muslim world.

Due to the unexpected and surprising military victories of the tiny State of Israel, many Arab nations now claim that it is not the total annihilation of the state of Israel they are after, but rather, their goal is to liberate the lands Israel occupied in the aftermath of the Six Day War of 1967.

Officially, the terms 'occupation' and 'settlements' have since become the buzzwords by which to denote, to decry and defame Israel's control of the territories across the 1967 armistices lines; ignoring the fact that before their attack on Israel, on March 8th 1965, the Muslim world had one goal and one goal only: the complete and total annihilation of the Jewish State. Egyptian President Gamal Abdel Nasser proclaimed: *"We shall not enter Palestine with its soil covered in sand. We shall enter it with its soil saturated in blood."* May 16, 1967, *"The existence of Israel has continued too long. We welcome the Israeli aggression. We welcome the battle we have long awaited. The peak hour has come. The battle has come in which we shall destroy Israel."* - Cairo Radio. A day later, on May 17, *"All Egypt is now prepared to plunge into total war which will put an end to Israel"* - Cairo Radio. On May 20, 1967, General Hafez al-Assad, Syria's Minister of Defense, and later President, boasted: *"Our forces are now entirely ready.... to initiate the act of liberation itself and to explode the Zionist presence in the Arab homeland ...the time has come to enter a battle of annihilation."*

---

[3] To reiterate, unJews is a term used to describe secular liberal Jews in positions of power; i.e. government, justice system and the media.

On May 27, Nasser declared: *"Our basic objective will be the destruction of Israel. The Arab people want to fight."* And four days before the outbreak of war, on June 1, 1967, Iraqi President Abdul Rahman Ali (later killed by Saddam Hussein) threatened: *"The existence of Israel is an error which must be rectified. This is our opportunity to wipe out the ignominy that has been with us since 1948. Our goal is clear - to wipe Israel off the map."* On May 28th, Gamel Nasser at a press conference declared, *"The existence of Israel is in itself an aggression..."* and President Aref of Iraq added *"The existence of Israel is an error which must be rectified. This is our opportunity to wipe out the ignominy which has been with us since 1948. Our goal is clear - to wipe Israel off the map."*

Keep in mind that creation of a Palestinian state was definitely not their aim! And it hasn't been since. Therefore, it is not Israeli aggression but the series of unprovoked Arab attacks that lead to the events which precipitated Israel's takeover of territories across the 1967 frontiers -an act of clear legitimate anticipatory preemption and self defense against that aggression. Clearly the main Arab contention against Israel has nothing to do with land, one specific border or another, or even the 'right' of the conjured Palestinian people to establish an independent country -a twenty-third Arab state. It is the mere existence of Israel that has been and currently is being rejected by the majority of the Muslim world.

In order to understand were this hatred came from, we must take a step back and look at some historical facts that will clarify much of what we have just read.

"I am a Palestinian, but don't like the name.
Palestine is a name the Romans gave Eretz Yisrael
with the express purpose of infuriating defeated Jews"
GOLDA MEIR
Prime Minister of Israel, (1969~1974)

THE JEWISH STATE

Shortly after the British relinquished control over the land, the Jewish residents of Palestine declared their independence and the creation of the new State of Israel. Contrary to expectations, the Jews, outnumbered and overpowered managed to survive the war that was waged against them by the Arab world. But it a major turning point in modern Israeli history was the unexpected and overwhelming Israeli victory of the Six Day war in 1967. The Arab-Israeli conflict as we know it was a consequence of that victory and succeeding political events that shaped current affairs in Israel. Before we go into a more detailed history of the rebirth of Israel, allow me to set the stage by pointing out how some of these political realities came to be. You might be unfamiliar with a few of the players I will mention below, and even with some of the historical events that have lead us to where we are today, but before I flood you with historical data, I believe it is necessary to present an authentic Jewish perspective of today's political situation.

"We are close to achieving peace" - say the 'New Zionists', or as they are referred to in some academic circles, the 'progressive Israelis'. They have been telling us this for decades. 'Peace Now,' a radical left-wing organization founded in 1978 (emphasis on the word 'Now'), has pressured Israel to submit to painful concessions that have achieved, well... much except peace. They of course blame others for not being able to bring about this 'peace' they promise. But left-wing governments have been in control of Israel in more than one occasion and even when they are not directly elected to office, they continue playing a crucial part in directing Israel behind the scenes, and in accordance to their idyllic model.

The year is 1989 and Shimon Peres and his associates sneak out of Israel, leaving behind then Prime Minister Yitzhak Shamir to deal with a hard-to-please James Baker, who is not just any anti-Semite, but he is Secretary of State for President George H. Bush. Shamir fenced valiantly, but behind his back, Shimon Peres, Yossi Beilin, Uri Savir and a few other ideologues of the far left, set out to find Israel's new peace partners and bring home the longed for solution to the Arab-

Israeli conflict. Peres has the conditional support of Egypt who gladly signed a peace deal with Israel back in 1978. Egypt, after being vanquished in war, got land and riches in return for a promise of peace, official recognition of Israel's existence and a commitment for socio-economic collaboration[4]. President Hosni Mubarak promises to support Shimon's bold move.

Next in line is Mauritania, a small African Muslim nation. Peres signs them on and nails it with promises of technological and economic assistance, again, in exchange for 'peace and recognition'. So off he goes to Jordan. King Hussein, Abdullah's father and predecessor, in desperate need of water and commercial incentives receives a plentiful promise from Peres and his associates, and Jordan too is in. The next step is to fly Yasser Arafat, the head of the Palestinian Liberation Organization, from his hideout in Tunisia into Israel with the purpose of having him lead the pseudo-Palestinian people into statehood.

Shimon Peres needs one more player to seal his dream plan: Syria, Israel's most feared enemy on its northern border. Since being defeated in the Shalom HaGalil war (1982), Lebanon becomes a proxy state of Iran via the terrorist organization, Hezbollah, so it is Syria that Peres so desperately needs to step forward and help forge his New Middle East dream into existence. But Syria demands Israel cede the Golan Heights, Israel's tallest mountains and main source of water[5].

Meanwhile in Israel, Shamir loses the following elections and Yitzhak Rabin, a highly decorated general, becomes Prime Minister in 1992. Shimon Peres is appointed Foreign Minister and helps Yasser Arafat secure complete autonomy over Gaza and Jericho with promises of much more in the near future.

Everything is working out for Mr. Peres, except for that one issue involving Syria. The world waits to hear from Syria's dictator. Will Hafez Al Assad[6] have the guts

---

[4] Camp David Accords, 1978
[5] From the Golan there is a clear view of all of Syria, representing a key military advantage. Also, rain water flows from the Golan into the Kineret (Sea of Galilee), which is Israel's main source of water.
[6] Hafez al Assad was the father of the current President and dictator of Syria, Bashar al Assad.

to break-off from Iran and join Peres's dream world? Will Syria join in the ranks of Egypt, Mauritania and Jordan and recognize the existence of Israel? Will they give up their proud anti-Israel stands? The Arab world pressures Syria not to agree to any formal truce, and since the destruction of Israel was and still is part of their agenda, Assad remains undecided.

It takes a lot of groveling, bargaining, begging and prostrating, but Israel counts with the best pleaser and appeaser in the entire Middle East. Shimon Peres goes at it and with the support of Russia, France, Great Britain and the U.S. somehow gets Syria to agree to become part of his Five-country 'peace pack'. Peres comes closer than ever before to realizing his dream of creating a 'New Middle East': A dreamed up world where Israel would be reduced further in size but supposedly will survived based on commitments and promises of peace and commerce from the world community, and the protection of the United Nations.

Suddenly, Prime Minister Yitzhak Rabin has a change of heart! Yitzhak Rabin, being a military general, understands the gravity of giving up control of the Golan Heights to Israel's second most feared enemy. Without the Golan Heights there is a good possibility that Israel's scarce water supply will be cut even further. Its mountains will again be used as launching pads for rocket and sniper attacks against civilians in Israel's northern towns as they had been prior to 1967. Rabin tries to convince Peres that Syria has nothing to offer Israel except for empty promises. Syria thrives mostly on the opium and heroin trade, and the hosting and export of terrorism. Rabin explains that Syria, even if it signs a peace treaty, will gladly take over the Golan Heights but ultimately will continue to submit itself to Iran's will. Yitzhak Rabin crushes Peres's dream of forging his New Middle East, and refuses to acquiesce.

Forty-five days later, Yitzhak Rabin, Israel's Prime Minister, is shot dead.

How can anyone assume that crushing Shimon Peres's dreams had anything to do with Rabin's demise? We are told to attribute this perfectly timed assassination to coincidence. Maybe so. But let's take a moment and look at the whole picture.

Shortly before Rabin's assassination, Shimon Peres's plans included the need to convince Israelis that giving land away to 'Palestinians' is a necessary yet "painful sacrifice." His main obstacle, besides convincing the Israeli public to go along with this, is figuring out what to do with the Jews living in those areas. Peres begins planting fear in the hearts of the Israeli public. He pursues his goals by utilizing two commonly accepted lies: First, that transferring Arabs out of Israel is Nazi-like behavior and that will get Israel ostracized from the world community, and second, that Arabs represent a social threat to the Jewish State, asserting that the Arab birthrate –a demographic demon- will bring about the end of the Jewish State by democratic means.

(Shimon Peres and Yasser Arafat)

The Left argues that transferring Arabs is nothing short of Nazism. How can Jews do to Arabs what Nazis did to Jews no that long ago? It didn't matter that there is absolutely no commonality between Jews in Europe and the Arab residents of the disputed territories. Peres is an expert in semantics and manipulation and therefore convinces the public that the only possible remaining solution is to transfer the Jews out instead. This will certainly bring about virtually no resistance from the world community, no outrage from human rights groups, no opposition from foreign governments, no UN condemnations. The world is by now convinced that the Jews stole the land from the Arabs, therefore, Jews being thrown out of their homes in order to 'help' procure a peace with the 'Palestinians' is seemingly the 'just' thing to do. It will not only educe silence from those who whether it had been the other way around would have screamed 'bloody murder', but on the contrary, the world leaders will give their wholeheartedly support to such an endeavor.

In Israel however, it will not be so easily accepted. Peres needs to figure out a way to throw Jews out of their homes without encountering too much internal opposition. Since most of the Jews of the West Bank are not 'progressive Israelis' but rather religious pioneers, he figures it will not be too hard to alienate them from their fellow Israelis who seem to be striving for a more modern and liberal society. The world's political players are in a rush to get things moving. The Jewish settlers need to be demonized in the eyes of the public. Both the media and the Ministry of Education, tools of Israel's liberal elite, jump on the bandwagon with the full support of the secular judicial system.

Although settlers had been admired and supported since the inception of the state in 1948 and prior, the media and many secular educators begin hammering into Israel's minds, that settlers are nothing but ultra right-wing religious fanatics that need to be removed in order to bring about that longed-for peace. Newspapers, radio shows, politicians and professors, begin promoting the idea that it is because of these settlers that Arabs hate Jews and carry out attacks on Israeli civilians across the country. The settlers, according to them, are the real reason there is no peace in the land.

Even the international media (TIME, Newsweek, The New York Times, and others) demonize Jewish settlers with ease of mind. No journalist prior to this period would have ever thought of writing a story about a place they had never been to, about people they had never met, or about events to which they had no knowledge of. With enough political push from the powers that be, journalism becomes fiction! A mixed multitude of Arabs become 'Palestinians', terrorists become militants, victims become oppressors, and settlers become fanatics.

Muslim terrorist groups step it up a notch. An apparent endless supply of suicide bombers begin blowing themselves up in Israeli buses, restaurants, and shopping malls. The gory images and the collective pain are overwhelming. The public is angry and is looking for the reason this is happening, and demanding a proper political and military response. Rabin calls Jewish victims of Arab terror, "sacrifices for peace"; the public is outraged.

Among the most outspoken opposition to Rabin's government are religious and Zionists Jews who call on the military to strike back hard against terrorists, even at the expense of tumbling down the political efforts Foreign Minister Peres. To make sure religious Jews, many of whom are settlers, are perceived in the worst light possible, Shimon Peres turns to Avi Dichter, the head of the Mossad -Israel's secret service. Dichter, a man who had always been unfriendly to religious Jews , recruits one of his trainees, a young man by the name Avishay Raviv. He asks Raviv to infiltrate a group of right-wing 'extremists' and incite them to go beyond the limits in order to depict them as radicals and irrational.

Raviv participates in anti-government rallies and befriends young activists. In order to gain their trust he creates a poster of Rabin dressed up as an SS Nazi officer. Even the most ardent religious settlers would not dare go that far, and as much as Rabin is disliked and even hated by some for giving up Jewish land to the 'Palestinians', that poster crosses all boundaries. Raviv immediately creates other posters and signs reminding the Jewish public that Rabin had played a commanding role in the killing of the Altalena Jews. The incitement grows like wildfire. Raviv is welcome into a group of protesters who are clueless of his true identity and that of those behind him. Raviv becomes appraised of their every move and behind the scenes, none other than Shimon Peres is manipulating it all.

On November 4th of 1995, Yigal Amir fires two shots at Rabin's back at point-blank range.

Amir, a young passionate law student from Herztliya , is a member of the group that Raviv 'coincidentally' has infiltrated. A video is released showing Amir shooting Rabin twice in the back after leaving a peace rally in Tel Aviv. It seems to have been a straightforward murder. However, a few questions are raised after the event that demand clear answers. A five-minute walk to the hospital takes twenty-two minutes by car even though most streets are cordoned-off. No explanation is given for this delay. Dr. Gutman, the first physician to see Rabin, together with other hospital witnesses including doctors and nurses, states that Rabin had been brought in with three bullet wounds, two in the back and one in the front. Several other inconsistencies and strange events occur that night and are brought into question but the government quickly takes control of the situation. In the end, it is Peres who assumes the position as Prime Minister and Peres the one who releases the 'official' version of the events. Amir is arrested and charged with premeditated murder. The public stands no chance of ever knowing the whole truth regarding Rabin's assassination.

It takes seven years after Rabin's murder for the court to call on Avishay Raviv to testify on the matter, and lo and behold, they not only hold a closed-room session but the findings remain secret and forever sealed. Carmi Gillon, another one of Peres's shady colleagues, fearing Raviv would say something incriminating awaits the judge's decision in Denmark thus steering clear from possible deportation. And this is but one more example of the nervousness that surrounds the ever more suspicious involvement of the government in the brutal assassination of Israel's Prime Minister.

No one can prove or state with certainty that Peres had Rabin killed in order to propel his New Middle East dream. But as long as the judicial system in Israel continues to act like a criminal syndicate, we will never know the truth. Even if we dislike conspiracy theories, the lack of transparency especially in this matter does not ease anyone's suspicions.

As Peres readies to serve the Golan Heights on a silver platter to President Assad, he loses the elections to Benjamin 'Bibi' Netanyahu. At least temporarily, Shimon's dreams are put on hold.

The events described above give you but a glimpse of the rift that exists between the nationalistic Jews and those refer to as the unJews. Religious and traditional

Zionist Jews differ drastically with those that describe themselves as pragmatic and modern. Most of the Jewish people disagree with the likes of Mr. Peres who has a perverted and unpopular idea of what Israel should be physically and spiritually. Unlike him, who personally saved Arafat's life on more than one occasion, most Jews would have gladly put a bullet in the head of that bloody terrorist. Peres and his followers did a disservice of widening the gap between the religious and the secular in an already conflicting country. Worst of all, in his well-advanced age, he continues to make damaging remarks and plan dangerous compromises with world powers that have Jewish interests at the bottom of their list[7]. Even when Peres ceases to be, others of his same caliber have already taken possession of powerful positions in Israel that will make it very hard for any elected officials to effect any significant change without their seal of approval. The likes of Ehud Barak, Manny Mazus, Dorit Beinish, and the slick Yossi Beilin, will make sure that no Netanyahu and no Avigdor Lieberman, Aryeh Eldad or any other remotely right-wing member of parliament ever get to enact what they were elected to do.

The Ministry of Education continues to strive for the demonization of religion and settlers set forth by its predecessors, yet polls show that Israeli youth is hard to deceive. There is a tendency to the right that defies the best efforts of Peres and his design. When Arabs scream *'death to the Jews'*, when they launch terrorist attacks and fire rockets into Jewish towns, it is hard to buy into the propaganda that dominates the Israel's media, educational system, courts, police force, academia, political elites, and even our military leadership. The popular voice is diametrically opposing. When Syrian forces can massacre 130,000 men, women and children to put down a revolt to overthrow their dictator, and the UN quietly goes about its business, but suddenly screams bloody murder when Jews want to build homes in Jerusalem, then the people have no alternative but realize that those in power are nothing but anti-semitic thugs. And that includes many Israelis that within our government and state act as their enablers.

---

[7] President Shimon Peres plans to tell Arab leaders that the overwhelming majority of Israeli citizens favor a return to the 1949-1967 borders, according to *Maariv*. May 24th, 2013.

It is difficult to answer why someone like Shimon Peres who helped Israel in many worthy endeavors such as the building of Dimona and the acquisition of nuclear energy and weapons, would then turn 180 degrees and become one with Israel's enemies and accusers. I honestly cannot figure it out. Gaius Sallustius Crispus, Roman historian and politician, (86 BCE-c.35 BCE) once said: "*Ambition drove many men to become false; to have one thought locked in the breast, another ready on the tongue.*". The same thirst for power affected Menahem Begin, Yitzhak Shamir, Ariel Sharon, and even Benjamin 'Bibi' Netanyahu. Since the signing of the Oslo accords and the murder of Rabbi Meir Kahane and Rehavam Ze'ev Gandhi, no Jewish leader has been able to stop this self-destructive trend.

I now invite you to look at the history of the creation of the modern state of Israel, and thus gain a better understanding of the issues surrounding the seemingly endless Arab-Israeli conflict.

Note that I have written this book as a second part to a religious discourse presented in a book entitled '*The Answer, Does Religion Really matter?*' I believe that it is impossible to understand the current situation in the Middle East if one thinks that the Arab-Israeli conflict is only about a territorial dispute. To think that this conflict is about land, occupation, racism, apartheid or any other nonsensical media-based and political jargon is to play into the hands of those who for so long have taken advantage of the prevalent ignorance of the majority of the world's audience. Make no mistake, this conflict has all to do with religion, and although Israel is a secular state, it is its 'Jewish character' that has the Arab world up in arms.

For two thousand years Jews wondered around the world; communities found solace for years or decades at a time, but mostly endured expulsions, persecutions, and mass deportations. If and when Jews were allowed to settle quietly it was mostly with the understanding that they were nothing but second-class citizens, and as long as they paid the higher taxes they were allowed to "live". The moment Jews began enjoying real 'equality' as they did in Germany, Hitler's Third Reich managed to move the Christian masses of Europe to slaughter mercilessly a third of the Jewish people. It is this slaughter and the persecutions that Jews have endured for so long that propelled the re-establishment of the Jewish State. Thousands of Jews managed to return (or rather flee) to Palestine and rejoin their brethren that for centuries had only a miserable existence in an otherwise desolate land.

Much of what you are about to read deals with the historical background to the Arab-Israeli conflict. It is important to know the truth about the re-establishment of the State of Israel. Many Jews seem not to know all of the facts and therefore fall prey to those who accuse Israel of being a foreign occupation and an illegitimate entity -a description most fitting of the current Muslim usurpers. Knowledge is a powerful weapon. Knowing the facts will enable you to respond to the false claims that have plagued the mainstream media and much of the liberal academic world.

Who of Israeli or Palestinian leaders were born in Palestine?

ISRAELI LEADERS:
BENJAMIN NETANYAHU, Born 21 October 1949 in Tel Aviv.
EHUD BARAK, Born 12 February 1942 in Mishmar HaSharon, British Mandate of Palestine
ARIEL SHARON, Born 26 February 1928 in Kfar Malal, British Mandate of Palestine
EHUD OLMERT, Born 30 September 1945 in Binyamina-Giv'at Ada, British Mandate of Palestine.
ITZHAK RABIN, Born 1 March 1922 in Jerusalem, British Mandate of Palestine.
ITZHAK NAVON, Born 9 April 1921 in Jerusalem, British Mandate of Palestine.
EZER WEIZMAN, Born 15 June 1924 in Tel Aviv, British Mandate of Palestine.

ARAB PALESTINIAN LEADERS:
YASSER ARAFAT, Born 24 August 1929 in Cairo, Egypt
SAEB BERAKAT, Born April 28, 1955, in Jordan. He has Jordanian citizenship.
FAISAL ABDEL QADER AL-HUSSEINI, Born in1948 in Bagdad, Iraq.
SARI NUSSEIBEH, Born in 1949 in Damascus, Syria.
MAHMOUD AL-ZAHAR, Born in 1945, in Cairo, Egypt.

THE RE-ESTABLISHMENT

According to biblical accounts, Abraham first set foot on the land of Cana'an over four thousand years ago. But it wasn't until 500 years later that his descendants came back from Egypt, where they had been enslaved, and took possession of the land. Since then, there has been a constant Jewish presence in Israel, sometimes in larger, and sometimes in smaller numbers, depending on the conquering forces who temporarily asserted their dominion. In terms of the existence of an independent country, there has never been one except for the kingdoms of Israel and Judea established 3,300 years ago; kingdoms that were eventually defeated by the Babylonians and subsequently by the Roman Empire. There has never been a country called Palestine, and the land that today encompasses both Jordan and Israel carried that name which was given as a symbol of Roman victory. It was the empire's intention to erase the names of Israel and Judea from the face of the earth. Ironically, it was the Romans who disappeared in the annals of history.

The word Palestine derives from "Plesheth", a name that in English appears frequently in the Bible as "Philistine". Plesheth, is a general term meaning migratory. These migrants invaded and conquered Israel's southern coastline. The Philistines were neither Arabs nor Semites; they were most closely related to the Greeks. They did not speak Arabic. They had no connection, ethnic, linguistic or historical with Arabia or Arabs.

From the fifth century BCE, Greeks called the eastern coast of the Mediterranean "the Philistine Syria" using the Greek language form of the name. In 135 CE, after putting down the Bar Kochba revolt, the second major Jewish revolt against Rome, Emperor Hadrian wanted to blot out the name of the Roman "Provincia Judaea" and so renamed the land "Provincia Syria Palaestina", this was the Latin version of the Greek name and the first use of the name as an administrative unit. The name "Provincia Syria Palaestina" is later shortened to Palaestina, from which the modern, anglicized "Palestine" is derived.

Although Jews find themselves homeless for 2,000 years, their yearning to return to the land of Israel never diminished. The land barren and desolate, awaited their return.

In the 1800's, one Tisha B'Av[8] as Napoleon walks through the streets of Paris he hears bitter wailing coming from inside a building. When he walks in he sees a group of Jews sitting on the floor reciting poems from the book of lamentations (*kinot*) and crying. He asks them, "Why are you crying?" They answer that, "Jerusalem is overrun and the Temple destroyed." Napoleon thinks for a minute and then tells the Jews, "Do not worry, it is just an untrue rumor. I know for a fact that all is quiet in the Middle East." The group then explains to him that they are mourning an event that took place 1,800 years earlier. An astounded Napoleon replies, "If you are still crying 18 centuries later, I have no doubt that one day your temple will be rebuilt."

History did away with the Romans and the Roman Empire while Jews, although exiled from their land, somehow managed to survive. And although it takes close to 2,000 years, the Jewish people are finally able to return to their cherished homeland.

1312 BCE - 660 CE

Israel is first a country in 1312 BCE, two thousand years before the founding of Islam. Jews rule the land for a thousand years thereafter and continue to have a presence in the land for 3,300 years, mostly while under the rule of various conquering forces.

After the Arab conquest of Palestine in 635 CE, their control lasts only 22 years and even then, Jerusalem is not made their capital. Jerusalem has nothing to do with Islam or Islam's dominion, and Jerusalem is never mentioned by name in the entirety of the Qur'an. In contrast, Jerusalem is mentioned 669 times in the

---

[8] Tisha B'Av is commemorated every year as a day of national mourning for the Jewish people.

Bible, not taking in to account the 161 references to Zion. In addition, Jerusalem is mentioned by name 154 times in the New Testament, for a total of 823 times. So from where does the Islamic claim to Jerusalem come about?

Muslims will claim that there is one allegoric mention of Jerusalem in their holy text. The Qur'an refers to Muhammad's alleged "night journey" (*isra*). The story goes as follows: "Glory to (Allah) who did take his servant for a journey by night from the Sacred Mosque to the farthest mosque..." Surah 17:001. When this Surah is revealed in the year 621 CE approximately, the Sacred Mosque already existed in Mecca, but where was "the farthest mosque?" It is apparently identified with places inside Arabia, either in Medina, or in a town called Ji'rana, about ten miles from Mecca, which Muhammad visited in 630 CE. Palestine had not yet been conquered by the Muslims, and contained not a single mosque!

It is in the year 635 CE that Arabs enter the land of Israel. Their desire to claim a connection to the land that both Jews and Christians considered holy, leads to imaginative twists and creative interpretations. A connection is necessary if they are to claim Islam as being an update to the Old and New Testaments.

THE UMMAYAD DYNASTY (661 CE - 750 CE)

The first Ummayad ruler, Mu'awiya, choses Jerusalem as the place where he ascends to the caliphate, and he and his successors engage in a construction program in the city: religious edifices, a palace, and roads. They effectively treat Jerusalem as their unofficial administrative capital.

The Ummayad Caliph, from 688 CE to 691 CE, builds the Dome of the Rock right on the spot where the Jewish Temple had stood centuries before. Then, in 715 CE, in order to build up the prestige of their dominions, the Umayyads build a second mosque on the Temple Mount, and call this one 'the farthest mosque' (al-masjid al aqsa). With this, the Umayyads retroactively give Jerusalem a role in Muhammad's life, and insert Jerusalem post hoc into the Qur'an, thus making it more important to Islam. If "the farthest mosque" is in Jerusalem, then

Muhammad's "night journey" and his subsequent ascension to heaven (*mi'raj*) also must have taken place on the Temple Mount. Convenient indeed.

Being that Muhammad's alleged "night journey" takes place in 622 CE, he dies in 632 CE, the Dome of the Rock is built by Amir Abd-ul-Malik in 688-691 CE, and Masjid al-Aqsa is built in 715 CE, then, what mosque did Muhammad visit, enter and pray at, before ascending to heaven? Seeing that the Qur'an mentions an alleged journey of Muhammad's to a mosque that did not exist during his lifetime, how should this be interpreted?

No matter what acrobatics Islam will perform in order to give some convoluted and fantastic answer to their claims, what is important to note is that no country is ever established in the land of Israel. It is only as a result of their success at historical revisionism and brainwashing the world with the 'big lie' of a Palestinian people, that Palestinian Arabs have more recently began to claim that they are the descendants of the Philistines, and even the pre-historical Canaanites. As if that myth were not enough, their leadership has claimed that "Palestinian Arabs are descendants of the Jebusites"[9] displaced when King David conquered Jerusalem. They also argued that "Abraham was an Iraqi" and "Jesus was a Palestinian." Here, they were correct, but left out a very important part - Jesus was a Palestinian Jew!

In 1750 the Ummayads are displaced to internal warring factions, and Islam engages in a long struggle against the Christian church in battles known as The Crusades.

751 - 1700

The land of Israel remains mostly desolate and the population centers minuscule. In the north there are malaria-infested swamps and in the south an inhabitable desert. Still, a number of Jews manage to survive in that harsh environment mainly through charitable contributions from communities abroad.

---

[9] Yasser Arafat. Speech in Ramallah to int'l delegation Jun 1989.

Nevertheless, since the days of the Caliphate to the 1700's and until about 200 years ago there is a Jewish majority in the land of Israel. Even as Christian Crusaders engage in battles against the Muslims, the Jews manage to avoid some the violence and maintain a presence in their war-torn land.

Three hundred years ago marks the beginning of a dramatic shift in population which gives rise to the complex Arab-Israeli conflict of today.

1701 - 1897

In the mid-17th century there is an important Aliyah (immigration) of Turkish Jews, though many left due to the lack of resources, opportunities, and a subsequent outbreak of Malaria that claims many lives. In terms of large numbers of people flocking to the land of Israel, a group of 1,500 Jews from Europe, headed by Rabbi Judah Hasid, settle in Jerusalem in the 1700's.

The first organized Aliyah consists of a group of Hassidim (Orthodox Jews) lead by the disciples of the Ba'al Shem Tov. They come to Israel in 1764 followed by the students of the renowned 'Gra' in the early 1800's. Rabbi Elijah ben (son of) Shlomo Zalman, often referred to as the "Vilna Gaon" -Genius from Vilna-, or simply the 'Gra,' is born in 1720 in Lithuania. He is convinced that it is a Torah (Biblical) obligation for every Jew to return to the Holy Land, and exhorts his followers to move to Israel. He himself attempts a trip, but for unknown reasons, never makes it farther than Germany. The Gra dies in 1797. Nevertheless between 1800 and 1812, groups of his students and their families, numbering over 500, settled in the land of Israel. These students first live in Tzfat (Safed) in northern Israel, because the Ottomans restrict Ashkenazi (European) Jews, from moving to Jerusalem. However, following an earthquake and shortly after an outbreak of the plague, in addition to persecution by the Ottoman and Druze residents, they succeed in having the ban lifted and many families are able to move to Jerusalem.

The Hassidim establish the neighborhood of Mea Shearim, today an ultra-orthodox enclave in Jerusalem. Not only Jews but Arabs as well, come to Israel in small numbers. Unlike the Jews, Arabs do not come out of an ideological yearning but rather, because they are ordered to. From 1517 to 1916 Turkey's Ottoman Empire controls a vast empire, a portion of which is today Lebanon, Syria, Israel and Jordan. Ibrahim Pasha, the ruler of the Ottomans, wants to strengthen his position in the area and brings thousands of Turkish Arabs to Jaffa and other areas of Israel. Even so, the Ottomans never claim Israel as being a legitimate part of Turkey.

There are never any calls for independence on behalf of the Arab newcomers. No attempt or interest in the creation of a country, state, or even an autonomous entity. The Arabs and the Jews work together, they peacefully co-exist, and it is known and accepted that although the Ottomans rule from afar, they are all living in a land referred to as Palestine, which had been home to the Jewish people and the Jewish people alone.

1898 - 1945

At the beginning of the twentieth century there are between 100,000 and 148,000 Arabs in the land of Israel and a smaller number of Jews, approximately 40,000, that had been there for generations. The exact number of Arabs is hard to track since many are Bedouins who migrate from one place to another; others are Turkish who travel back and forth -a benefit of belonging to the ruling Ottoman Empire.

During World War I (1914 - 1918), Turkey pledges its allegiance to Germany. When Germany is defeated, so are the Turks. In 1916 control of the southern portion of the Ottoman Empire is "mandated" to France and Britain under the Sykes-Picot Agreement, which divides the region (practically the entire Middle East) into zones of imperial domain. Lebanon and Syria are assigned (mandated) to France, and 'Palestine' (today's Jordan and Israel -including the 'West Bank') is mandated to Great Britain.

The accusation that Israel is a creation of the British colonialists is ironic, since most of the Arab states owe their origins to the entry and domination of the European powers. Prior to World War I, the Arab states of Iraq, Syria, Lebanon, and Jordan did not exist, but were only districts of the Ottoman Empire under different names. They became separate states as a result of European intervention. The most infamous of all came to be as a result of the British placing an Arabian Hashemite family in power over the greater part of Palestine, and calling it 'Transjordan'.

Furthermore, Saudi Arabia and the smaller Gulf states emerge from treaties that their leaders sign with Great Britain. By means of those treaties, the British recognize the legitimacy of local Arab families to rule what become states like Kuwait, Bahrain, and Qatar. A similar British treaty with the al-Saud family in 1915 set the stage for the eventual emergence of Saudi Arabia in 1932.

Meanwhile, the Jewish effort to revitalize the land of Israel creates jobs and opportunities and sparks a greater migration of Arabs entering the land of Israel. Now that the British government rules the land, the leaders in the highest echelons of government and society begin pondering with the idea of granting Jews their independence. The British receive a mandate by the League of Nations (United Nations) to establish a "Jewish state" in what today constitutes Israel and Jordan. Great Britain reluctantly agrees.

The Jews begin transforming the malaria-infested swamps, the rocky dry land, and the unfriendly desert to prepare for the re-birth of Israel. Unconvinced that this is in the best interest of the British Empire, the imperialist rulers begin impeding Jewish immigration contrary to their previous commitment to international agreements.

There is never any attempt by the Jewish residents to "rid" the land of the Arabs that had been there for decades, not even of those Arab masses that immigrated seeking work alongside the Jews. Survival and development seemed to be a common goal for all the residents that willingly or not, had come under British rule.

Before the League of Nations[10] imposes a re-partition of the land called Palestine, the same land the British had taken over from the Ottoman Empire, Israel consisted of an area of 46,000 square miles extending to both sides of the Jordan River. In 1922, Britain, with the approval of the League of Nations, partitions the land in two unequal areas. East of the Jordan River they establish a new country and call it Transjordan, a land comprising of 77 percent or 36,000 square miles of what should have been part of the Jewish national homeland. And west of the Jordan river they assign to both Arabs and Jews with plans of an added repartition. In 1922 the British hand over Transjordan to an Arabian family called the Hashemites.

Between 1917 and 1924, after the collapse of Ottoman Empire, Hussein bin (son of) Ali rules an independent area on the west side of the Arabian Peninsula called Hejaz. This self-proclaimed king of the Arabian clan of Hashim has five sons. Ali, who briefly succeeds him to the throne of Hejaz before its loss to the Saud family; Abdullah, who later becomes the king of Transjordan (with the tacit support of the British Foreign Office), and whose descendants rule the 'kingdom' of what today is known as Jordan. Then there is Faisal, who is briefly proclaimed King of Syria, and ends up becoming King of Iraq. Next, there is Prince Zeid, who moves

---

[10] The League of Nations was renamed United Nations in 1945.

to Jordan when his brother's grandson is overthrown and murdered in a coup in 1958. Lastly, there is Hassan who dies at a young age.

The British give semi-autonomous control of Transjordan to Abdullah who proclaims himself a king and who later changes the name of his new kingdom to Jordan (Transjordan was hard for them to pronounce). Notwithstanding the fact that the land Abdullah is now ruling over had been previously designated by the League of Nations to become the Jewish national homeland, he makes sure to rule fearlessly, quickly getting rid of anyone who might question his power. King Abdullah rules over a peasant native majority who had lived there for centuries and who never had any national aspirations. To this day there is a clear differentiation between the Hashemites and the native Arabs -also referred to as Palestinians. Ironically and unlike their counterparts within Israel, most Jordanian Arabs are truly Palestinian, and in Jordan, these non-Heshemites, enjoy second-class citizenship at best.

In 1923 the British cede the Golan Heights to the neighboring French Mandate of Syria while the remaining 23% of the its mandate in Palestine is repartitioned once again to create both a small and indefensible Jewish State and an additional Arab country for the multi-cultural mix of Arab immigrants and residents. Jews are subsequently barred from settling anywhere in Transjordan (Jordan) and from returning to the Golan Heights and other regions in northern Israel. Even Nahariya and other Galilean areas are excluded from the suggested Jewish homeland according to this new ill-intentioned plan of Great Britain's imperialist forces. In 1929 feeling the tacit support of the British, Arab murderers massacre the Jews of Hebron, hundreds more are murdered in Tsfat (Safed) and dozens more are killed in Jerusalem all under the 'watchful' eyes of British soldiers. Their lack of regard, which became the standard for the United Nations, begin turning the desperate Jewish hope for a homeland into a distant and seemingly unattainable dream.

Arab murderous assaults on Jews are occurring before the establishment of any legitimate state, setting up a precedent for future attacks.

Secular Jews who arrived in the early 1900s filled with socialist ideas of emancipation, begin working hand-in-hand with the British authorities. These Jews, referred to as 'establishment Jews', settle mostly in places that generate the least amount of controversy, namely in what constitutes central Israel, Tel Aviv and its surroundings.

However, not all Jews share this need for compliance. Three main Jewish rebellious groups, the Irgun, Etzel and the Lehi begin retaliating against the Arab marauding gangs and at the same time, opposing British control of Palestine. In the late 1930's and early 1940's Jewish survivors of the Holocaust begin pouring in. The British acquiescing to Arab demands establish a quota, limiting the number of Jews that are allowed to enter Israel. Boatloads with thousands of survivors, Jewish men, women and children, are mercilessly sent back by the British forces to concentration camps in Europe were many are systematically exterminated by the Germans and the Poles. British hatred of the Jews and the idea of a Jewish state repulse them so much so that they do all they can to be in the way of Zionism and the Jewish dream of a homeland.

Many clandestine boats are smuggled into Palestine by both the revolutionaries and the establishment Jews - who although acquiescing to British demands, manage to put together a militia called the Palmach. During WWII, Nazi Germany, their allies and their collaborators, murder most of the Jews of Europe.

In conjunction to those massacred at the hands of Stalin in Russia and the Kazaks in Ukraine, it amounts to a third of the entire Jewish people.

There is no question that the British, although at war with Germany served to further the genocidal goals of the Nazis and assist in the murder of Jewish refugees. In Israel, they allow Arabs to violently harm the Jewish residents, while making it illegal for Jews to defend themselves. The Arabs make an alliance with Germany lead by the Mufti of Jerusalem, Mohammad Amin al-Husseini (Haj Amin). Using the turmoil of the Arab Revolt as cover, al-Husseini consolidates his control over the local Arabs with a campaign of murder against Jews and non-compliant Arabs, the recruitment of armed militias, and the raising of funds from around the Muslim world using anti-Jewish propaganda.

(Mohammad Amin al-Husseini and Adolf Hitler y"sh)

In 1937 the Grand Mufti expresses his solidarity with Germany, asking the Nazi Third Reich to oppose the establishment of a Jewish state, to stop Jewish immigration to Palestine, and to provide arms to the local Arab population. He visits numerous death camps and encourages Hitler to extend the "Final Solution" to the Jews of North Africa and Palestine.

Since the alliance of the Arabs with the Nazis is aimed against Jews and not Great Britain, the British deliberately ignore the increasing animosity and anti-Jewish violence of the Arabs towards the Jews. Liberal or conservative, religious or not, Jews are left with no choice but to fight for their survival.

The Lehi, also known as the "Stern Gang", is the most anti-British of the four major Jewish underground movements. While the Palmach, and even the Irgun support the British during their campaign against Germany in World War II, the Lehi begins to fight against British colonialism in Israel. It is only after the war, that the Irgun joins the clandestine warfare against the British. In 1942 British officers find Yair Stern, the founder of Lehi, in his hideout. They handcuff him, and then shoot him to death. Stern is 35 years old.

"We are at war against the occupier. And we are far from hesitation in regard to an enemy whose moral perversion is admitted by all."
Avraham 'Yair' Stern

1946 - 1967

In 1946, after Jewish rebels bomb the King David hotel -a building used by the British as their military headquarters-, the British consider leaving Israel for good. On April 16, 1947 Dov Gruner, Yehiel Drezner, Eliezer Kashani, and Mordechai El'kachi are hanged while singing Hatikvah (Israel's national anthem).

On April 21, Meir Feinstein and Moshe Barazani blow themselves up using an improvised explosive device hours before their scheduled hanging. And on May 4, one of the Irgun's largest operations take place - the raid of the prison in the citadel of Akko. Twenty-three men commanded by Dov "Shimshon" Cohen carry out the operation. The surprise explosion of the prison's wall allows 41 underground members to escape. Some are killed in the escape, and three of the fighters - Meir Nakar, Avshalom Haviv, and Yaakov Weiss - are caught and sentenced to death.

Shortly after the bombing of the Akko prison, the British announce they are leaving Palestine for good. The Establishment Jews that had been collaborating with Great Britain [11] take control, and in spite of their differences, the revolutionary Jews are asked to join in the struggle for the creation of an independent Jewish State. As soon as David Ben-Gurion, Israel's first Prime Minister, declares the establishment of the new Jewish State on May 14th 1948, Israel's Arab neighbors announce that a *Jihad* (holy war) is about to take place. They tell the Arabs who resided in Israel, close to 180,000 men, women and children, to leave their homes and head east to Jordan temporarily. In the unfriendly hills of the West Bank they are to wait for Israel's destruction, and then they will be able to return to their homes and partake of the spoils of war.

The five largest Arab armies of the world unite with the determination to destroy the newly born State and the resolve to throw the Jews into the sea. War brakes out almost immediately after Ben Gurion's declaration of independence.

---

[11] That collaboration included at times giving up the hideouts of rebel Jews, knowing well that their fate would be death by hanging.

The Allied Powers support the creation of the State of Israel for the sole purpose of facilitating the extermination of the 600,00 Jews who dodged the gas chambers. After all, British military experts estimate that the Jews will hold out against the combined military intervention by the Arab states for only three days. They all impose an arms embargo on Israel, which they enforce strictly but supply arms freely to the Arabs. The Brits release German POW officers from prisons to command the Egyptian army.

The Jewish people are still divided between those who support the establishment Jews who control the military wing of Palmach and those who support the revolutionary Jews of the Irgun and Lehi. The revolutionaries make a large purchase of weapons, mainly from the French. They try smuggling these weapons in a boat they rename Altalena. Nearly 1,000 Jewish immigrants from places as remote as Cuba, are aboard. Prime Minister David Ben-Gurion proposes to create a unified army made up of the Palmach soldiers together with the revolutionaries. At the same time, in order to assert his power, he orders soldiers of the freshly formed Israel Defense Forces to fire not on Arabs fighters, but on fellow Jews -those smuggling weapons in the Altalena.

The Irgun, a Zionist faction led by Menachem Begin, is unaware of Ben Gurion's intentions. As the Altalena approaches the Israeli coast, the troops of the Palmach come down to the shore to prevent the unauthorized unloading of the boat. Begin, not willing to give over all the supplies that his group had purchased and brought in at their own expense, tries negotiating with the Palmach commander, none other than Yitzhak Rabin.

Light artillery is aimed at the boat and casualties are reported, but the soldiers on the Altalena, do not fire upon their Jewish brethren who are shooting at them, hoping that they would come to their senses. The Palmach begin shelling in the direction of the Altalena, each shell coming closer and closer. The captain of the boat hoists the white flag, but he is ignored. Finally, the boat is hit and sinks. Nineteen Jewish soldiers are killed and many more are wounded. All the supplies and armament is lost. Ben-Gurion publicly praises the "holy canon" that sank the Altalena as if he had been victorious in some kind of military confrontation; while the truth is, once again the Establishment Jews betray the revolutionaries in order to maintain control of the newly born State. Keep in mind that all this is happening in the middle of a war against Arab armies.

The Palmach and the Irgun finally decide to join forces and fight off the incoming Arab armies, they soon begin fending off and keeping the Arab armies from overpowering the newly formed Israel Defense Forces. Jews are heavily outnumbered and everyone who is able to pick up a weapon is ordered to fight. Then the war comes to an end. Although the Arabs are unable to destroy Israel, certain territorial Arab victories take place. Jordan invaded Israel and seized Judea and Samaria -the areas known as the West Bank- and the old city of Jerusalem. The Arab residents that had followed orders from their fellow Arab brethren soon find themselves stuck in Judea and Samaria in large makeshift encampments referred to as Refugee Camps and under Jordanian rule. Others get stuck in the south, in what constitutes the Gaza strip under Egyptian control. It is a bloody war, but after 2,000 years, Jews finally have a State of their own once again.

An additional consequence of Israel surviving the war of Independence is the aftermath endured by the Jewish communities of Middle East. Massive deportations of Jewish citizens of Arab nations take place. They are expatriated without their possessions or any form of compensation. It is open season on the Jewish communities across every Muslim country.

Arab rioters engage in bloody pogroms. Zionism becomes a capital crime. Looting and persecution causes 850,000 Jewish men, women and children to migrate to Israel. The Jewish communities in the Middle East come to near extinction.

Jews in the Arab World

	1948	1958	1968	1978	2011
Algeria	140,000	130,000	1,500	1,000	1,500
Egypt	75,000	40,000	1,000	400	100
Iraq	135,000	6,000	2,500	350	7
Libya	38,000	3,750	100	40	0
Morocco	265,000	200,000	50,000	18,000	4,000
Syria	30,000	5,000	4,000	4,500	100
Tunisia	105,000	80,000	10,000	7,000	1,500
Yemen/Aden	63,000	4,300	500	500	250
Total	851,000	469,060	69,600	31,790	~7,500

Taking advantage of the lack of supervision by the United Nations or any other independent entity, Jordanians desecrate whatever holy and religious sites remain for Jews and Christians in and around Jerusalem. Tombstones from Jewish cemeteries are used to pave roads and as urinals. The Western Wall becomes a municipal garbage dump. Arab refugees are granted Jordanian citizenship (second class, of course) and are told that someday soon the Arab world will rearm and attempt again at driving the Jews into the sea. Then, they would gloriously return to their homes inside Israel proper.

In a similar manner, in the south, Egypt takes control of Gaza and the Arab refugees therein. While in the north, Syria takes control of the Golan Heights; a region that soon becomes their key platform for terrorist attacks against the agricultural communities of the Galilee.

A second attempt in 1956 brings together the most powerful Arab armies of the Middle East once more against the still young Jewish state. Small, almost insignificant territorial gains on behalf of the Jewish state come as a result of yet another Jewish victory. From 1948 to 1967 the Arab refugees on the West Bank live under Jordanian rule. Not once do any of the local Arab population plead for the creation of a new country or ask for any kind of independence. Not once does it even occur to them to create a 'Palestine' in the West Bank or demand autonomy of any kind. Similarly, from 1948 to 1967 Egypt controls the Gaza strip, and not once do any of these 'Gazan' Arabs (mostly Egyptian in origin) ask for independence, autonomy or even claim to have a different or distinctive identity from their Egyptian brethren. Arabs, whether in the West Bank or in Gaza, have only one thing in mind, to wait, re-arm and eventually destroy the Jewish state. Then in 1967 it becomes evident that another war is brewing. Arab threats of annihilation fill the airways once more.

"Those (Jews) who survive will remain in Palestine. I estimate that none of them will survive." Ahmed Shukairy, chairman of the PLO in Jordanian Jerusalem

War erupts, the Arabs have the upper hand, but God has plans that dramatically differ from the Arab desire to obliterate the Jewish State. Miraculously, Israel is able to defeat the powerful Arab armies, liberate Judea, Samaria, Gaza and the Golan Heights, defying every prediction of her impending doom. Not until after the 1967 war do the Arabs in the West Bank and Gaza begin claiming those lands as their own. Arab refugees in Israel both in the West Bank and in Gaza begin to identify themselves as 'Palestinians' two decades after the establishment of modern Israel. The term Palestinian until then, had been associated with both Jews and Arabs that had lived in Israel prior to 1948, and even so, it never had a connotation that symbolized belonging to a different nation, other than Israel.

Countless miracles take place during the Six Day war of 1967. Still, the army generals are all secular Jews, many slightly anti-religious; and among them, Yitzhak Rabin and Moshe Dayan. It is Moshe Dayan that directs the liberation of Jerusalem and sees the Arab residents of the West Bank flee to Jordan[12]. Religious Jews are ecstatic to have been able to stand after 2,000 years of exile, once more, on the same spot were the ancient Jewish Temples once stood. The Arabs of Jerusalem, knowing the humiliation that they have caused the Jews, have no doubt that the Israelis will in a matter of hours destroy the Dome of the Rock and the Al-Aqsa Mosque that Muslims had built purposely on the same spot that is holy to the Jews. They never expected what happened next.

Moshe Dayan, fearing that the Arab world would continue hating Israel, decides to relinquish ownership of the Temple Mount to the Arab Waqf (religious authority) as a token of peace and a good-will offering shortly after the cease fire is declared.

Dayan does not stop there. He orders Jewish troops to chase after the Arabs of the West Bank who are well on their way to entering Jordan, and beg them to return! Dayan fills the cities of Beth Lehem, Hebron, Ramallah, Jenin, Kalkiliya, Nablus (Shechem) and others, with Arab refugees who later become known as

---

[12] Moshe Dayan has a different idea of what Israel needs to be and his understanding of the Jewish connection to Har HaBayit (Temple Mount) is not a priority.

'Palestinians'. They never, not for an instance, appreciate Israel's gestures. On the contrary, they continued wholeheartedly to support Arafat and other terrorists in their war against the Jewish state.

Moshe Dayan's surrender of the Temple Mount is the biggest and gravest blunder that can be attributed to the Jewish people since the sin of the Golden Calf.

Dayan, perpetuates the fiction of the Palestinian people and the false concept of 'refugees'. From the 100,000,000 refugees that were relocated and absorbed worldwide since the Second World War, the Arabs of Israel (the so-called Palestinians) are the only group of people left adrift. in contrast to these so-called Palestinians, the UN ignores the plight of Jewish Sephardic refugees totaling some 850,000 men, women and children who had also been forced to flee Arab lands when their host countries begin stepping up violence, persecution and pogroms against them. They were quickly absorbed in war-battered Israel, a country no bigger than the state of New Jersey. To Jews, no compensation, no apology; as if no crime had ever been committed.

1968 - 1973

The Arab nations are less than pleased with the territorial gains made by Israel. Not only did they lose valuable territory in terms of military advantage points but it is a blow against Islam and their national sense of pride. The fight is not over.

On October 6, 1973 while the Jews fast and attend the religious services of Yom Kippur (the Day of Atonement and the holiest day in the Jewish calendar), Egypt and Syria open a coordinated surprise attack against Israel. On the Golan Heights approximately 180 Israeli tanks face an onslaught of 1,400 Syrian tanks. Along the Suez Canal, 80,000 Egyptians attack fewer than 500 Israeli defenders. At least nine Arab countries, including four non-Middle Eastern nations, actively aid the Egyptian-Syrian war effort. During the war, an Iraqi division of some 18,000 men and several hundred tanks is deployed in the central Golan. Iraqi MiGs operate over the Golan Heights. Algeria sends three aircraft squadrons of fighters and bombers, an armored brigade and 150 tanks. Approximately 1,000-2,000 Tunisian soldiers are positioned in the Nile Delta. Sudan stations 3,500 troops in southern Egypt, and Morocco sends three brigades to the front lines, including 2,500 men to Syria.

Besides serving as financial underwriters, Saudi Arabia and Kuwait commit men to battle. A Saudi brigade of approximately 3,000 troops is dispatched to Syria, where it participates in fighting along the approaches to Damascus. Also, Libya sends Mirage fighters to Egypt (from 1971-1973, Libyan President Muammar Qaddafi gives Cairo more than $1 billion in aid to rearm Egypt and to pay the Soviets for weapons delivered). Once again, the Jewish State proves too much for the Arab world.

End The Unjust Jewish Occupation of Muslim Land!

(sic)

1974 - 1982

Even though it is due to the efforts of the Irgun and the other right-wing revolutionary groups that the British had been forced to leave Israel, it was the appeasers and opportunists of the Hagana and the socialist Bundt (Jewish Establishment) who form a political and governmental infrastructure. Even so, they invite the religious and right wing groups to join them in the establishment of the new State of Israel. Right-wingers are kept in secondary positions for many years and under a very short leash controlled by the liberal judicial system.

It is David Ben-Gurion, Isaac Weitzman, Golda Meir, Moshe Dayan, Yitzhak Rabin and Shimon Peres who establish and formalize what came to be known today as Medinat Israel (the State of Israel). Two main political parties are formed: Labor, a dovish left-wing party with most of the figures mentioned above, and Likud, a supposedly hawkish right-wing party with members of what had been the Irgun and the Lehi -who were now either under pressure to collaborate or voluntarily in cahoots with the ruling party.

The Labor party leads Israel through wars victoriously, and Arab terror is answered with Jewish terror and tough military responses. It is the Likud, the so-called right-wing party, which signs the first part of the process of self-destruction, that is, the infamous Camp David Agreements where Israel is to relinquish control and sovereignty of the Sinai Peninsula to Egypt in exchange for peace. The government of Israel sends its top military general, Ariel 'Arik' Sharon to dismantle and force Jewish settlers out of the Sinai so it can be given away free and clear. The settlement of Yamit is destroyed. Israel relinquishes the Sinai Peninsula and capitulates to the pressures imposed on it by the then American president, Jimmy Carter (an anti-Semite par excellence).

Menachem Begin, Israel's Prime Minister, does not even insist for Egypt to take control of Gaza and its Egyptian inhabitants (the Palestinians of Gaza). The entire Sinai, its mineral riches, oil wells, beautiful beaches and other natural resources, are all given away in exchange for a insincere promise of peace and a tongue-in-cheek recognition of Israel's existence.

Golda Meir, a left-wing politician of the avant-garde, and the first female Prime Minister of Israel, (also a non-observant Jew), is always clear to the fact there is no Palestinian people, but the Likud in 1977 officially recognizes and legitimizes the so-called Palestinian Arabs. It is the Likud, under former Irgun leader Menachem Begin, who pushes Israel to take its first step towards making suicidal concessions.

From one moment to another, the thousands of Arabs who immigrated to Israel from virtually every country in the Arab world and northern Africa, and who joined up with the small number of natives, become a 'national' entity. A people must start sometime and somewhere, and that could be considered a legitimate foundation, except that they all claim to be descendants of the native Turks and Bedouins of the land; and that it is they, not the Jews, who have a legal and historical right to the land of Israel[13]. The Likud legitimize these people without rebutting their false claims, giving credence and political standing to this new no-longer fictitious and usurping entity.

UPDATE:
It's been over 30 years since that dreadful day and there are neither economic nor social exchanges with Israel's former enemy. Anywhere in Egypt, in any elementary or high school one may visit, in any geography book one may open, the State of Israel still does not appear! A very strange peace indeed!

Egypt is the largest recipient of funds and military aid from the US and has been amassing the largest army in the Middle East. Poverty is widespread, but apparently the need to be militarized is a priority for a government with no official enemies. One can only wonder.

---

[13] This includes all of Israel – from the Mediterranean to the Jordan river and from the Golan Heights to Eilat.

For what it's worth, from the signing of the Camp David Accords, there is relative calm until the PLO steps up their struggle by attacking Israel from Lebanon. How the Palestinians end up in Lebanon is a consequence of their actions in Palestine, by that I mean, Jordan.

The Palestinian Liberation Organization (PLO) gradually builds up what amounts to their own virtual state within Jordan. They control the refugee camps and begin to smuggle in weapons undermining King Hussein's authority. In September 1970 Palestinian terrorists fly two hijacked planes to Jordan and blow them up. At that point, Hussein's forces fearing a coupe, attack the Palestinian camps. Hundreds are murdered. Men, women and children are killed without a second thought. Yasser Arafat survives the attack that came to be known as Black September. He takes his followers and move to Syria.

Assad understands that these 'Palestinian' terrorists represent a threat to his power as well and manages to push the PLO to its new camp ground: Lebanon. The PLO takes over the south and slowly creeps inside Beirut. Once called the 'Paris of the Middle East', Beirut becomes the headquarters of the world's most unscrupulous terrorists. Lebanon, a Christian country, is too weak to repulse the invasion.

In March 1978, PLO terrorists infiltrate Israel. They hijack a civilian bus shortly after murdering an American tourist walking near an Israeli beach. When Israeli troops intercept the bus, the terrorists open fire and a total of 34 hostages are killed in the attack. The IDF retaliates by attacking terrorist bases in Southern Lebanon but before they can inflict significant damage, they allow the United Nations to intervene. As always, UN troops are unable to stop terrorism and are incapable of preventing their re-arming.

In 1981 a greater threat hovers over Israel. Saddam Hussein, the dictator of Iraq, finalizes the building of a nuclear reactor and is close to developing nuclear weapons. Menachem Being, notwithstanding opposition from Shimon Peres, gives green light to the IAF who immediately carries out an operation to bomb the reactors. The mission is a success and the world is outraged at Israel's blunt unilateral decision to attack Iraq. Arab terrorists resume their assault from the north. These continuous terrorist attacks give start to the First Lebanon War which formally erupts in 1982. During this war, Israel attempts to eradicate the PLO from Lebanese soil. Many Israeli soldiers lose their lives when these Arab terrorists decide to enact the use of suicide-bombers. PLO terrorists film the attacks and air the videos. The Israeli public is incensed and voice their disappointment with the Likud's lack of proper response.

In the following elections, Labor comes into power but by a slight margin. They in turn focuses its efforts not in fighting the new threat from Lebanon, but rather in diminishing the influence of Judaism over Israeli secular life; this in order to strengthen its constituency. In the late 70's and early 80's Education Ministers Shulamit Aloni and Amnon Rubinstein make every effort possible so that Israel will raise secular Israelis in its schools instead of "religious troublemakers", thus guaranteeing that in the future, the Likud becomes second at best.

The rift between the secular and the religious grows farther apart. Jewish students are taught officially that indeed, the Arab claims that Jews had taken possession of their land, are accurate. Religious Jews are associated with anti-progress and even anti-peace and are called parasites of the state. Arab terror escalates and a greater sense of 'Palestinian' identity grows among the Arab residents across Israel, even in the midst of the Arab towns who enjoy full social and economic benefits. Arab citizens see themselves as Palestinians more than ever before, and their numbers increase. Their proclivity for large families threatens to overtake Israel by numbers if it not by force. Ironically, Palestinian identification grows with the support of Israeli liberal groups who encourage their quest for independence. Betzelem, Yesh Gvul, Peace Now and Women in Black become the voice of the 'oppressed palestinians' ignoring truth, facts, objectivity and most of all, the Jewish legitimate claim to the land of their ancestors.

Rhetoric from Labor leaders as well as other leftist politicians make the public fear of further acts of terror, increase their support of efforts to appease the world powers. Fearing what the left might do, and knowing what they are capable of, in 1982 right wing Israelis manage to gain a slight majority and elect the 'right-wing' Likud party to lead the country. In hope of a strong response against the increased wave of violence, Yitzhak Shamir, an ex-Lehi (Stern Gang) leader surprises the nation. His 'response' to Arab terror is the issuing of rubber bullets and pepper-gas canisters to Israeli soldiers and policemen. Shamir's concern is to avoid upsetting the world; and the Intifada grows like wildfire across the country. Shamir's fear of world condemnation only fuels the zeal of the Arab nationalists and their supporters. For the first time there is a strong anti-Israel sentiment that thanks to the media, is felt worldwide.

Terrorists sprout everywhere. Amateur young Arabs resort to murdering with knives and axes. Organized and well-funded terror groups work with explosives and execute well-crafted terror operations one after the other. More Jewish lives are lost. Violence escalates with a series of PLO attacks and the resulting Israeli reprisals. The PLO has a force of some 15,000 to 18,000 members encamped throughout southern Lebanon. Approximately 6,000 fighters are foreign mercenaries from Libya, Iraq, India, Sri Lanka, Chad and Mozambique. The UN does nothing to stop the rearming of these terrorists and Israeli intelligence warns of the arsenal the enemy has acquired, which include mortars, Katyusha rockets, antiaircraft missiles and hundreds of T-34 tanks, courtesy of the Syrian army and the Russian military.

Although Israel has enough reasons to go to war with the PLO it takes one final provocation to induce the IDF into action. In June 1982 a Palestinian terrorist group led by Abu Nidal attempts to assassinate Israel's Ambassador to Great Britain, Shlomo Argov. The IDF subsequently attacks Lebanon driving out the terrorists in operation 'Peace for Galilee.' The IDF manages to capture Yasser Arafat and his guerrillas and finally expels the PLO from Lebanese soil. Arafat and his terrorists are shipped to Tunisia which gladly accepts to host them.

1983 - 1991

War is officially over; sporadic terror attacks are reported across Israel. Yasser Arafat and the PLO have been officially defeated, but that does not stop left-wing radicals Yossi Beilin and Shimon Peres form flying to Tunisia to attend secret meetings and plan the resurrection of the exiled arch-terrorist. They device a plan to save their 'political pawn' from extinction and inevitable oblivion. Arafat is by now bankrupt and his following is scattered and weakened by insurgency. If not for Peres and his entourage Arafat would have disappeared into the annals of history as a defeated murderer and terrorist. And although there is a law in Israel which forbids any official from contacting members of terrorist organizations, Peres and Beilin unilaterally decide to make of arch-terrorist Arafat their new 'peace partner,' and thus revive Shimon Peres's New Middle East fantasy. Shamir turns a blind eye to what it is clearly and legally an act of treason. Anti-Semites across the world under the guise of political leaders give their financial and overt support to this initiative. There is a deafening silence from the majority of the successfully brainwashed Israeli public when the news leak into the media.

(Shimon Peres and Yasser Arafat)

Four years of terror attacks and limited responses go by and tensions are running high once again. In 1987, the first Intifada finally brakes out. West Bank Arabs organize terror attacks against Israeli population centers while sending their teen-age children and their women to throw rocks at Israeli soldiers, policemen, and civilians traveling on main roads adjacent to Arab villages and cities. They know that Israeli soldiers will have a hard time using violence against them. The media acts as an enabler while demonizing Jews and blaming them for Arab violence! The false notion that Israel is an apartheid regime and that Arabs are being oppressed begin to spread worldwide. Israel's PR machine is dead; the Arab moguls overpower it. The world media is supported by the UN. Of the 175 UN Security Council resolutions passed before 1990, 97 are directed against Israel. Of the 690 UN General Assembly resolutions voted on before 1990, 429 are directed against Israel. Israel-hatred spreads like wildfire.

In response to Arab terror and claims of Arab rights to the land of Israel, Rabbi Meir Kahane, an outspoken right-wing rabbi, establishes his political party Kach ("thus" in Hebrew). He is a proponent of inducing Palestinians to leave the West Bank voluntarily; if they refuse to leave, Kahane advocates expelling them. He believes Orthodox Judaism should be the official state religion, and claims that Israel has strayed away from the Jewish character it was originally intended to have. In 1984 Rabbi Meir Kahane becomes a member of the Israeli Knesset when his party Kach gains one seat in the Parliament. Jews all across Israel, and from all walks of life, suddenly realize that Rabbi Meir Kahane's proposition of a population transfer has become more than mere rant. Kach intends to position the tiny Jewish state with a sound advantage to offer a peace treaty to its Arab neighbors without resorting to life-endangering compromises. And although the idea of mass deportation and population transfer does not sit well with the majority of Jews -due to obvious references to deportations suffered in Russia and across Europe during the Holocaust- Arab violence is making his suggestion evermore desirable, reasonable and even necessary.

Rabbi Kahane responds to a United Nations resolution that equates Zionism with racism:

"A certain resolution on Zionism has been passed at the United Nations. In reality, it is a resolution on Judaism. It is important that a reply be given. It is important that the world know precisely what Zionism is and what the Jewish people are: It is

important that the nations hear our proclamation: Listen world; I am Zionist, I am a Jew!

And listen too, Jew. Listen so that you will understand yourself who you are and what and why. For there is no escape from it even if one should be so foolish as to desire to flee the greatness and majesty of the Jewish destiny. Listen so that you will be able to stand proud and tall and know what to reply with dignity and not hesitant defensiveness. So that you will know from where you came and to where you go, without the former to is impossible to know the latter.

Our feet are standing within thy gates O Jerusalem - and they will never leave. This is Zionism, and the Untied Gentiles call it 'racist' and debate how to take my city away from me. Foolish world; sooner will the sun fail to rise tomorrow. The Jews have come home to their Zion and have welded their city together with a fierce tightness that none least of all the humor that is the United Nations can sunder. A people which patiently bides its time for millennia will not easily - ever - give up its state and capital."

Rav Kahane's words reverberate. His books are being widely distributed and his ideas are reaching farther than expected. Jews, who would otherwise vote for Likud, are now attracted to Kach. Rabbi Kahane's ideology has no appeal to the Jews of the left, so in reality Kach does not represent a threat to the Labor party. It is in the Likud's immediate interest to stop Rabbi Kahane on his tracks or risk losing the greater part of its constituency. Rabbi Kahane's choice of words sometimes paints him as an extremist. He threatens to destabilize the entire system of government and demands fierce and violent action against Arab terrorists and rioters.

"If you love your people, you must hate Arabs, and not because they're Arabs, but because they're enemies. Even if those who hate you are Chinese, you hate those who hate you - unless you're crazy or stupid.

Know this, that they are your enemies and they don't love you, and just as they will
have no mercy on you, have no mercy on them. Said HaKadosh Baruch Hu (God): Go
out against them as enemies. Just as they do not have any mercy on you, do not
have any mercy on them."

Rabbi Kahane's public appearances and publications are waking Jews up. The
Likud is estimated to be reduced by half in the following elections if they fail to
take action against the Kach party. Moreover, the world powers are also not
pleased with Rabbi Kahane's propositions. In 1986, through illegal maneuvering
Kach is declared to be a racist party by the Israeli judicial system and banned
from running for the Knesset. It does not matter that members of Kach are
Ethiopians, Moroccans, Yemnites, together with Europeans, American
immigrants and natural born Israelis. What's more, followers of Rabbi Kahane
span the religious gamut, from atheists to ultra-orthodox and everything in
between. The only commonality among Rabbi Kahane's followers is a deep
seeded love of Israel and the certainty that the Arab enemy must be expelled.
However, the ideology is considered extremist and the Likud uses illegal means
to get rid of its competition, and it does so with the support of both Israel's left-
leaning judicial system, the media and the international community. It is not a
matter of what is better for Israel, but how can the current political powers
maintain their control over the country in spite of Arab aggression and popular
discontent.

In 1988 both Israeli Arabs and those living in the 'disputed territories' (West
Bank and Gaza) realizing that Kahane is no longer a threat, begin rioting and
demanding Israel give them autonomy. The PLO for the first time, demands to be
allowed to create an autonomous state of their own, one within Israel's
sovereign borders. Due to the poor living condition of many of these Arabs -still
under the label of refugees and perpetuated purposely by the Arab nations- they
are portrayed to the world community as being victims and underdogs. This
results in an unforeseen effort of the world community in pressuring Israel into
compliance. Threats of severe economic boycotts and the willingness to
transform Israel into a pariah state creates panic among Israeli politicians. Since

Israel is not yet self-sufficient and it depends on trade and commerce for its continued existence, Israeli diplomats -focused mainly in finances and not so much on survival- begin making the 'Palestinian' dream a reality. Palestinians embark on a tougher campaign of terror with the sole objective of pressuring Israel into compliance.

Rabbi Kahane's party is declared illegal, however, he vows not to stop campaigning, and continues to disseminate his ideas both in Israel and abroad. Rabbi Meir Kahane travels to America to both fundraise and increase awareness of the need to support Israel. One night in Manhattan in a New York City hotel, after concluding a speech calling on American Jews to immigrate to Israel, an Arab, disguised as an orthodox Jew, shoots Rabbi Kahane mortally wounding him. On November 5th 1990 Rabbi Kahane is assassinated.

Rav Kahane's assassination becomes a source of conflicting accounts. Nosair Al-Sayid who pulled the trigger is a member of Al-Qaeda, a then relatively unknown terrorist group. Rabbi Kahane's demise is timely and convenient especially for the members of the Likud who even after banning his political party continued to lose followers to the Rabbi's camp.

Sayid is thought by many to have been a mole for both the CIA and the Mossad (Israel's secret service). Sayid is not charged with murder after killing Rabbi Kahane in front of 300 people. He is captured a few blocks from the murder scene after a police shoot-out. Later that night, police arrive at Sayid's house and find two Middle Eastern men there: Mahmud Abouhalima and Mohammed Salameh. They are taken in for questioning. Additionally, police collect a total of 47 boxes of evidence from Sayid's house, including thousands of rounds of ammunition, documents in Arabic containing bomb making formulas, maps and drawings of New York City landmarks such as the World Trade Center; and details of an Islamic militant cell with mentions of the term "al-Qaeda," a relatively unknown group at the time.

Furthermore, they find recorded sermons by Sheikh Omar Abdul-Rahman, an Egyptian militant cleric, in which he encourages his followers to "destroy the edifices of capitalism" and destroy "the enemies of Allah" by "destroying their... high world buildings." Also found are tape-recorded phone conversations of Sayid reporting to Abdul-Rahman about paramilitary training, and even discussing bomb-making manuals. Videotaped talks of one Ali Mohamed delivered at the John F. Kennedy Special Warfare Center at Fort Bragg, North Carolina. Top-secret manuals also from Fort Bragg and even classified documents belonging to the US Joint Chiefs of Staff and the Commander in Chief of the Army's Central Command.

Ignoring all of this evidence, later that evening, Joseph Borelli, the New York police department's chief detective, publicly declares the assassination of Rabbi Kahane, the work of a "lone deranged gunman." He further states, "I'm strongly convinced that he acted alone... He didn't seem to be part of a conspiracy or any terrorist organization."

Investigators continue to ignore all evidence that suggests Sayid had not acted alone. District Attorney Robert Morgenthau, who prosecutes the case, later speculates that the CIA might have encouraged the FBI not to pursue any other leads. Sayid, it was later found, worked at the Al-Kifah Refugee Center, which is closely tied to covert CIA operations in Afghanistan. Although the CIA and the Israeli Mossad have always worked together, and it is clearly in the interest of many Israeli politicians to end Rabbi Kahane's career permanently, no evidence of a conspiracy becomes public.

Aftermath:
Sayid is acquitted of Rabbi Kahane's murder, though he is convicted of lesser charges. He denies his involvement with the CIA or Mossad. Abouhalima and Salameh are also released only to be later apprehended and convicted for participating in the 1993 bombing of the World Trade Center.

Rabbi Kahane's murder strengthens Likud's position, but the world powers are siding ever more with the 'Palestinian' cause. Shamir responds to world pressure by agreeing to meet the Palestinian representatives in what became known as the Madrid Talks of 1991. Shamir meets with American and Russian representatives to discuss giving more autonomy to the Palestinians and begins the process of unilateral concessions and appeasement.

Being that the voice of opposition has been silenced, Shamir capitulates, folds, and sells Israel short.

1992 - 1995

Israelis boots Shamir out of office and elects the revered and veteran military general, Yitzhak Rabin, as Prime Minister. He campaigns hand-in-hand with his number one adviser and manipulator, Shimon Peres. They build upon the Madrid Talks that Shamir had attended, and transform them into the biggest campaign of misinformation, secret dealings, and illegal negotiations. Yitzhak Rabin has a bit of a drinking problem. He had suffered from a few mental breakdowns but still manages to maintain a solid enough public image. Meanwhile Shimon Peres plans a systematic dismemberment of the greater part of the land of Israel, all without due process and without a referendum or the public's approval. It is enough for the Rabin and Peres team to have been voted in, for them to use this as a *carte blanche* to do as they please. Rabin and Peres fly to Oslo together with a Palestinian delegation that includes arch-terrorist, Yasser Arafat.

Somehow, by means I can't even begin to speculate about, they convince the world that the 'repented' arch-terrorist Yasser Arafat, head of the Palestinian terrorist organization -the PLO-, is a worthy recipient of the Nobel Peace Prize[14]. Not one, but three Nobel prizes are given to probably the three least deserving people in the Middle East. Rabin, Peres and Arafat walk away with the 'honors'.

Shortly thereafter, they sign the Oslo peace accords, and it takes them no time to come home and implement the conditions stipulated upon Israel in their delusional peace treaty. They open the jails and let Arafat's murderous bands[15] go free. They give them weapons and call them the Palestinian Autonomy Police Force.

Rabin, Peres, and Arafat make an agreement that Arafat's armed forces would comprise of no more than 9,000 inductees, and that any Palestinian under arms would first have to be vetted by Israeli intelligence to ensure that he does not have a background in terror activity. From the beginning, the PA armed forces counted as many as 19,000 under arms and by 1995 they comprised at least

---

[14] Norwegian statesmen Kare Kristiansen resigned from the Nobel Prize committee because of the Nobel Prize bestowed upon Arafat. He told the Norwegian media that Peres had promised financial remuneration to fellow Nobel Prize Committee member Terje Larsen in order to ensure that he would share the Nobel Peace Prize with the late Prime Minister Rabin.

[15] Convicted terrorists of all degrees, some with life sentences that find themselves suddenly pardoned. Most later on become the Palestinian Police Force.

30,000. Since 1995, the IDF acknowledges that it no longer knows who has been recruited into the PA security force. Rabin and Peres arm an additional 40,000 Arab terrorists with Kalashnikov rifles and automatic pistols. Israelis are assured that this is the correct path to a permanent peaceful solution that will lead to coexistence. Doing this, Rabin claims, is an intelligent way of ending the bloody assaults of the 'Palestinian' Arabs.

Prime Minister Yitzhak Rabin on a press conference after a Knesset session tells the people of Israel the following:

"Stop being afraid. There is no danger that these guns will be used against us. The purpose of this ammunition for the Palestinian police is to be used in their vigilant fight against the Hamas. They won't dream of using it against us, since they know very well that if they use these guns against us once, at that moment the Oslo Accord will be annulled and the IDF will return to all the places that have been given to them. The Oslo Accord, despite what the opposition claims, is not irrevocable." -Yitzchak Rabin

Photo: Reuters

Yitzhak Rabin and Shimon Peres not only give recognition to Yasser Arafat and his terrorist organization (PLO), but they also ignore the tremendous waves of terror that overtake Israel thereafter. For the first time in Israel's history, the bloodshed of innocent Jews goes completely unanswered. Rabin calls the Jewish victims of Arab terror, "a necessary sacrifice for peace."

Arab promises of peace include a commitment to amend the PLO charter which refuses to recognize the right of Israel to exist. This and other unfulfilled commitments are exchanged for financial help, water, electricity and land concessions beyond the initial Gaza and Jericho relinquishments. Shimon Peres and Yitzhak Rabin free even more Arab terrorists from jail and promise Arafat that he will soon have a state of his own. Peres assures a battered Israel, *"It will be a long process, somewhat slow, but if all goes well, we will all benefit from this 'Peace Process' in the long run."* His promise never becomes reality.

Throughout 1994 and 1995 private agencies produce videos of Arafat's speeches where Arafat expresses support for Jihad to liberate Palestine: *"Kill a settler every day.... Shoot at settlers everywhere.... Woe to you if you let them reach their homes safely or travel safely on the roads.... Do not pay attention to what I say to the media, the television or public appearances. Pay attention only to the written instructions that you receive from me."* Peres implores the Israeli media not to air Arafat's speeches in the Arabic language. Peres also asks the US Congress not to view the videos of what Arafat was saying in Arabic. In December, 1995, Arafat invites Hamas, a recognized terrorist organization, to join his provisional regime. In 1996, Arafat appoints Hamas officials to run the religious departments and schools under his authority. Together with PA (Palestinian Autonomy) 'policemen' are also in charge of stopping Arab extremists from murdering Israeli citizens and army personnel. But it is precisely these so-called policemen, the culprits of many of the cold-blooded murders in Judea and Samaria, and the enablers of terrorists (including suicide bombers) who target Jewish civilians in Jerusalem and throughout the land.

Arab attacks become an every day occurrence. Suicide-bombers target buses, bus stops, restaurants, train stations, shopping malls, restaurants and markets. Hundreds of Jewish men, women and children are murdered in cold blood. The charter of the PLO is not amended. The insistence to continue to use terror as a 'legal' means of pursuing independence continues unchallenged. Rabin does not keep his word about disarming these terrorists. Not only are those guns not taken away from these Arab murderers, but to add insult to injury, Rabin and

Peres arm an additional 30,000 Arab terrorists with more Kalashnikov rifles and an assortment of machine guns after Arafat explains that he needs additional armed men to battle those who are against peace. Arafat makes a mockery of Rabin, the world powers and the people of Israel.

Rabin's naivety and *chutzpah* goes as far as to request from the American government to contribute to the training of a special sniper unit for the Palestinian Police. Arafat argues that he cannot stop suicide bombers without a proper sniper and special forces unit. Rabin receives America's blessing and commends his long-time collaborator and army general Ehud Barak to escort a select group of Palestinian Policemen to Virginia's CIA training camp near Langley. After completing their training these Arab policemen receive precision rifles equipped with scopes. These snipers are to shoot Arab terrorists and possible suicide bombers.

It is hard to believe that Rabin, Peres and Barak could be so gullible, but the alternative is for us to understand that they knew very well that these snipers not only would not ever shoot at their own, but that they would immediately turn their weapons against Jews. But why would Rabin and his gang not only allow but enable the murder of Jews? The truth is, in order to fulfill their promises to Arafat, Rabin and Peres had to find a way to transfer Jews from territories they promised to give away.

So long as the Jews being murdered are religious Jews from the 'occupied territories' (Judea and Samaria a.k.a. the West Bank, and the Gaza strip), the Israeli military response remains much more boo-ha than real. Some believe that Israeli leaders are being naïve, but since both Rabin and Barak have long military careers, it is hard to ignore the pressing reality: that in fact, they want to create an unbearable environment and pressure Jewish settlers to abandon certain parts of Israel, thus allowing politicians to propel their 'peace deal'. If successful, they will gain the world's approval, and substantial financial rewards.

Ironically, Rabin's conviction that Arabs would be better off being 'autonomous' is simply a consequence of his understanding that Jews and Arabs cannot really co-exist within the same country.

"I believe that in the long run, separation between Israel and the Palestinians is the best solution for resolving the Israeli-Palestinian conflict." Yitzhak Rabin

What he fails to appreciate is that giving Arabs one inch of Jewish land, leads them to understand that Israel as a whole, is up for grabs. The Arabs in Israel now more than ever, see themselves as having a chance to establish their dominion. They begin to spread the idea that Jews in Judea are illegal occupiers while Arabs from Arabia are actually indigenous! A lie that will reverberate for decades to come.

"The Oslo accords are a Trojan Horse; the strategic goal is the liberation of Palestine from the [Jordan] river to the [Mediterranean] sea" - Faysal Al-Husseini, Palestinian Authority Minister for Jerusalem Affairs.

On November 5, 1995, a Jew who opposes the liberal policies of the peace process assassinates the Prime Minister of Israel, Yitzhak Rabin. Many details about Rabin's assassination remain a mystery to this very day, as discussed in the previous chapter. Rabin's successor, Shimon Peres, vows to continue the work that Rabin allegedly pioneered.

1996 - 1999

With Rabin out of the picture Shimon Peres continues his campaign of deception. The Palestine National Council, meeting in April 1996, does not vote to nullify the PLO charter that calls for the destruction of Israel. However, Peres proclaims that Arafat has fulfilled his promise to amend the PLO charter, a lie that costs him the following elections. Israelis become so frightened by what Shimon Peres might do now that Rabin is out of the way, that they vote him out of government (proof that most Israelis are not completely insane). Peres receives the Arab votes and the votes of leftists and liberals, especially of those who are still sobbing over Rabin's assassination, but it isn't enough to beat Likud and Israel's new 'savior', Benjamin 'Bibi' Netanyahu.

This time the Likud will do the right thing! Or so it is believed.

This time Netanyahu will bring peace and security to Israel. That is Bibi's promise. Unfortunately, Israelis are proved wrong once again. Netanyahu meets with US President Clinton and the 'honorable' Nobel Peace Prize winner, arch-terrorist and murderer, Yasser Arafat; and just days after being elected, Prime Minister Netanyahu gives away control over most of Hebron to Israel's sworn enemy.

Prime Minister Netanyahu pledges further concessions and signs an Israel-Jordan Peace Treaty making Jordan only the second Arab nation to sign a peace treaty with Israel. This peace agreement with King Hussein of Jordan under the auspices of US President Bill Clinton means that Jordan recognizes Israel's right to exist. Israel in turn promises thousands of cubic meters of water from the Kineret, Israel's only lake and main water supply, parts of the Negev desert that Jordan had been disputing, and further promises to assist the 'Palestinians' and the autonomous organizations.

Regarding Judea and Samaria, Bibi initiates negotiations about percentages, which only opens the door to more unilateral giving and fraudulent 'negotiations'. His betrayal of the settlers causes him to lose the respect of the more hawkish members of his own party. His coalitions weakens. The Sephardic religious party (Shas) abandons their allegiance to the so-called right wing and in 1999 they help Labor regain power.

This time, former General Ehud Barak is elected and concedes to give away 95% of the West Bank plus parts of Jerusalem that had never before been contemplated by any Israeli leader. No referendum, no vote, a unilateral decision by a strong leftist government. It seems Israel is about to change forever. Things being what they are, Arafat, the murderer who never in his wildest dreams could have hoped for more, unexplainably refuses to accept this unprecedented and insanely suicidal unilateral offer. Israeli-Syrian peace negotiations fail as well when Hafez Assad rejects Barak's offer of the Golan Heights relayed by US President Clinton in Geneva. Ehud Barak, a creep that stands in a league of its own, is no less stunned than the rest of the Israeli public..

Arab terror activities increase. From the hills of Hebron which Netanyahu had relinquished irresponsibly to the PA (Palestinian Autonomy), a sniper terrorist takes aim at a baby carriage in a park with Jewish mothers and children. A ten-month old baby, Shalhevet Pass, is shot in the head and killed on the spot. No outrage. No world condemnation. Her murder and the subsequent murder of other Jews in the West Bank are mocked in the media. "We will not allow terrorist to destroy our efforts for peace" claim the politicians, paralleling

Rabin's declaration that murdered Jews are painful sacrifices for peace. Shimon Peres milks to the last drop the demise of Rabin, and declares his annual memorial a national day of mourning. What was a rift between the religious and the secular becomes a giant gap filled with anger and resentment. The feud between the two, takes a turn for the worse.

2000 - 2004

In the middle of the year 2000, Arab riots spread throughout Israel after Ariel Sharon visits the Temple Mount in Jerusalem . The second Intifada sees Arab 'policemen' join forces with Hamas, Tanzim, Fatah and Islamic Jihad terrorists. Israel's 'peace partners' in a long stream of terror, murder hundreds of Jewish men, women and children. Suicide bombers target civilians in buses, restaurants and shopping malls, while Arab snipers (the ones trained by the CIA under the supervision of Ehud Barak) claim dozens of Jewish lives in Israel's roads. Arabs are encouraged by their leadership to help fight the Zionist regime. Besides the organized acts of terror, Arab random attacks with axes and knives become a common occurrence. Among the hundreds of Jews murdered are Kobi Mandell, 14, of Tekoa, and his friend Yosef Ishran, 13, who are stoned to death while hiking near their home, south of Jerusalem. Their deaths begin to create awareness as to how dangerous Israel is becoming, and the direction political deals are pointing to.

Israeli police seem paralyzed. Arab terror is rampant. The people of Israel begin wonder who will come to their rescue? They call upon the Likud once more. Ariel Sharon after his gutsy display in Jerusalem convinces the Israeli public he will be the one to put an end to Arab terror! Sharon's leading role in the 1982 evacuation of Yamit (the Jewish settlement of the Sinai) is forgotten. Also ignored is the fact his two sons are involved in criminal activity. People know that Sharon is known to the Arab world as the 'Butcher of Beirut' a nickname he got during the 1982 Lebanon war when he, as acting General of the IDF, allowed the Christian militia to murder 'innocent' Palestinians in Sabra and Shatila (two

Palestinian refugee camps in southern Lebanon). Israelis hope that fear will serve as a deterrent.

In 2001 right-wing Likud leader Ariel Sharon is elected Prime Minister replacing Ehud Barak, and promises "peace and security." Israel then conducts operation Defensive Wall in Judea and Samaria following a large number of Palestinian suicide attacks against civilian targets. 2002 and 2003 are the bloodiest years in Israel's history. In 2002, 451 civilians are murdered including children that had been purposely targeted in bus bombings. In addition, 2,348 people are injured in attacks. In 2003, 210 people are assassinated and 1,123 are injured. Terrorists have the upper hand. Although disappointed but hoping that Sharon will live up to his reputation, in the 2003 elections Israelis give a wide margin victory (40 seats) to the right wing Likud party, returning PM Ariel Sharon for yet another term.

In 2004 Palestinian Authority President and arch-terrorist Yasser Arafat's health weakens by what some doctors claim to be leukemia; he is flown to France for treatment. Arafat dies in France shortly thereafter. Many speculate he succumbed to Aids, claiming he had been a long time pedophile. Some Muslims and sympathizers in an attempt to divert attention from the more plausible cause claim Israeli secret agents have poisoned him. (They seem to forget that it was Shimon Peres who saved Arafat's life repeatedly). Arafat's wife Suha is left with a multi-million fortune embezzled by Arafat himself from his international list of donors to the Palestinian cause.

Arafat left the world a legacy of terror.

A LEGACY OF TERROR

Yasser Arafat (1929-2004)

CAMERA, the Committee for Accuracy in Middle East Reporting in America compiled the following timeline of Arafat's life and accomplishments:

Born August 4th, 1929 in Cairo, Egypt and named Muhammad Abdel Rahman Abdel Rauf al-Qudwa al-Husseini is the fifth child of prosperous merchant, Abdel Raouf al-Qudwa al-Husseini.

In 1933 Arafat's mother dies. He and his infant brother are sent to live with their uncle in Jerusalem.

Late 1950's: Arafat co-founds Fatah, the "Movement for the National Liberation of Palestine."

January 1, 1965: Fatah fails in its first attempted attack within Israel -- the bombing of the National Water Carrier.

July 5, 1965: A Fatah cell plants explosives at Mitzpe Massua, near Beit Guvrin; and on the railroad tracks to Jerusalem near Kfar Battir.

1965-1967: Numerous Fatah bomb attacks target Israeli villages, water pipes, and railroads. Homes are destroyed and Israelis are killed.

July 1968: Fatah joins and becomes the dominant member of the PLO, an umbrella organization of Palestinian terrorist groups.

February 4, 1969: Arafat is appointed Chairman of the Executive Committee of the PLO.

February 21, 1970: Swiss Air flight 330, bound for Tel Aviv, is bombed in mid-flight by PFLP (a PLO member group) and 47 people are killed.

May 8, 1970: PLO terrorists attack an Israeli school bus with bazooka fire, killing nine children and three teachers from Moshav Avivim.

September 6, 1970: PLO terrorists hijack TWA, Pan-Am, and BOAC airplanes.

September 1970: Jordanian forces battle the PLO terrorist organization, driving its members out of Jordan after the group's violent activity threatens to destabilize the kingdom. The terrorists flee to Lebanon. This period in PLO history is called 'Black September.'

May 1972: The PFLP, part of the PLO, dispatches members of the Japanese Red Army to attack Lod Airport in Tel Aviv, killing 27 people.

September 5, 1972: Munich Massacre -11 Israeli athletes are murdered at the Munich Olympics by a group calling themselves "Black September", said to be an arm of Fatah operating under Arafat's direct command.

March 1, 1973: Palestinian terrorists take over the Saudi embassy in Khartoum. The next day, two Americans, including United States ambassador to Sudan Cleo Noel, and a Belgian diplomat are shot and killed. James J. Welsh, an analyst for the National Security Agency from 1969 through 1974, charges Arafat with direct complicity in these murders.

April 11, 1974: 11 people are killed by Palestinian terrorists who attack an apartment building in Kiryat Shmona.

May 15, 1974: PLO terrorists infiltrating from Lebanon hold children hostage in a Ma'alot elementary school. 26 people, 21 of them children, are murdered in cold blood at point blank range.

June 9, 1974: The Palestinian National Council adopts a "Phased Plan," which calls for the establishment of a Palestinian state on any territory evacuated by Israel, to be used as a base of operations for destroying the whole of Israel. The PLO reaffirms its rejection of United Nations Security Council Resolution 242, which calls for a "just and lasting peace" and the "right (of Israel) to live in peace within secure and recognized boundaries free from threats or acts of force."

November 1974: PLO takes responsibility for the PDFLP's Beit She'an murders in which 4 Israelis are killed.

November 13, 1974: Arafat, wearing a holster (he had to leave his gun at the entrance), addresses the U.N. General Assembly.

March 1975: Members of Fatah attack the Tel Aviv seafront and take hostages in the Savoy hotel. Three Israeli soldiers and three civilians are killed.

March 1978: Coastal Road Massacre -Fatah terrorists take over a bus on the Haifa-Tel Aviv highway and kill 21 Israelis.

1982: Having created a terrorist mini-state in Lebanon and destabilizing that nation, the PLO is expelled as a result of Israel's response to incessant PLO missile attacks against northern Israeli communities. Arafat relocates to Tunisia.

October 7, 1985: Italian cruise ship Achille Lauro is hijacked by Palestinian terrorists. A wheelchair-bound Jewish elderly man, Leon Klinghoffer, is shot and thrown overboard. Intelligence reports note that instructions originated from Arafat's headquarters in Tunis.

December 12, 1988: Arafat claims to accept Israel's right to exist .

September 1993: Arafat shakes hands with Israeli Prime Minister Rabin, inaugurating the Oslo Accords. Arafat pledges to stop incitement and terror, and to foster co-existence with Israel, but fails to comply. Throughout the years of negotiations, aside from passing, token efforts, Arafat does nothing to stop Hamas, PFLP, and Islamic Jihad from carrying out thousands of terrorist attacks against Israeli civilians. With Arafat's encouragement and financial support, groups directly under Arafat's command, such as the Tanzim and Al Aqsa Martyrs Brigade, also carry out additional terror attacks.

October 21, 1996: Speaking at a rally near Bethlehem, Arafat said "We know only one word - jihad! Jihad, jihad, jihad! Whoever does not like it can drink from the Dead Sea or from the Sea of Gaza." (Yediot Ahronot, October 23, 1996).

(Yasser Arafat with former US President Jimmy Carter)

April 16, 1998: In a statement published in the official Palestinian Authority newspaper Al-Hayat Al-Jadeeda, Arafat is quoted: "O my dear ones on the occupied lands, relatives and friends throughout Palestine and the diaspora, my colleagues in struggle and in arms, my colleagues in struggle and in jihad...Intensify the revolution and the blessed intifada... We must burn the ground under the feet of the invaders."

July 2000: Arafat rejects the peace settlement offered by Israeli Prime Minister Ehud Barak, which would have led to a Palestinian state.

September 2000: A new "intifada" is launched. Arafat continues to incite, support and fund terrorism.

July 2001: "Kill a settler every day.... Shoot at settlers everywhere.... Woe to you if you let them reach their homes safely or travel safely on the roads.... Do not pay attention to what I say to the media, the television or public appearances. Pay attention only to the written instructions that you receive from me." - Yasser Arafat, addressing his people at a public event.

January 3, 2002: Israelis intercept the Karine-A, a ship loaded with 50 tons of mortars, rocket launchers, anti-tank mines and other weapons intended for the Palestinian war against the Israelis. The captain admits he is under the command of the Palestinian Authority.

September 2003: IMF Report titled "Economic Performance and Reforms under Conflict Conditions," states that Arafat has diverted at least $900 million of public PA funds into his own accounts from 1995 - 2000.

November 11th, 2004: Arafat dies in Paris, France.

"We plan to eliminate the state of Israel and establish a purely Palestinian state. We will make life unbearable for Jews by psychological warfare and population explosion. We Palestinians will take over everything, including all of Jerusalem"
YASSER ARAFAT

In 2005 arch-terrorist Mahmoud Abbas, a founding member of the Palestinian National Liberation Movement (Fatah) -a terrorist organization dedicated to the destruction of Israel- is 'elected' President of the Palestinian National Authority. While Ariel Sharon plans a unilateral forced withdrawal of the Jewish communities of Gaza and northern Samaria, he suffers a massive stroke, leaving the leadership of Israel in the hands of the newly formed Kadima party (a mutation of the Likud, excluding its hawkish members) and lead by Ehud Olmert, a former Jerusalem mayor with a track record less than admirable.

In the summer of 2005 Israeli soldiers (mostly Beduins, Druze and secular Israelis) together with selected police forces from all over the country, begin evacuating Jewish settlers from Aza (the Gaza Strip) and northern Samaria (West Bank). Jewish men, women and children are forcefully dragged away from their homes. Their synagogues and community centers are emptied, as is their entire industrial and agricultural infrastructure. Their homes for over 32 years are destroyed not by Nazis, and not Arab armies, but by a politically driven and misguided Israeli secular force acting without national consent.

In a matter of days, not a single Jew is left in Gaza or northern Samaria. 10,000 Jews are left homeless. Many are placed in caravans and makeshift homes. After 30 years of living together, neighbors and family members are separated, bused out and dispersed across the country. Hundreds of Jewish soldiers are scarred for life from having to take part on this act of Jewish ethnic cleansing. Religious Jews who in the thousands come out and plead with soldiers and policemen to desist from committing what it is clearly a crime against humanity and the Jewish people, are left with a serious sense of abandonment and betrayal from their misguided countrymen. Hundreds of soldiers are imprisoned, a few commit suicide. Ultra-orthodox Jews also ignore the plea of their brethren. The religious national Zionists (*dati leumi*) are abandoned, belittled and defeated.

To understand how the public went along with this, we must look at the composition of Israel's society. In Israel, 8% of the population is considered Ultra-orthodox. They are not known for their Zionism or their willingness to interact with their fellow Jews, whether religious or not. For the most part they live in small enclaves and seem to care only about themselves. Some groups of Ultra-Orthodox are involved in acts of Chessed (charity) that benefit the broader community and some protest publicly only if a law or proposed change threatens to alter their way of life. Another 25% of Jews in Israel consider themselves modern orthodox and national Zionists. Many live in Biblical Israel, meaning in 'occupied territories'. They are known for their love and devotion to Israel and a resilient sense of Zionism. These Jews are involved in community service groups, outreach programs and are active politically and socially. The young men serve the army and are mostly found in combatant elite groups. Close to 100% of the Jews expelled from Gaza belong to this category.

Another 25% of Israelis consider themselves traditional (*mesoratim*). They have strong Zionist values and although they do not live a particularly religious life, they consider themselves very Jewish. Lastly and unfortunately, 42% of Israelis are secular. Some by choice but most are a product of decades of brainwashing by a secular, anti-religious Ministry of Education. Some secular Israelis consider themselves Zionists, but many do not. Some even form part of ultra left-wing groups that intentionally or not, support Israel's enemies. Seculars are known for supporting liberal causes such as environmental conservation, rights of homosexuals, social equality, etc. They do not care much for their religious compatriots, and if asked, they seem to support the 'two-state solution' to the

Arab-Israeli conflict even at the expense of their fellow countrymen. It is the majority of these Israelis who gave their support to Ariel Sharon's expulsion plan and Ehud Olmert's execution of the Gaza withdrawal.

Olmert's unilateral and lame attempt to appease Israel's enemies leaves open wounds that may not ever heal.

In 2006 the radical Islamist Hamas movement wins an upset victory in the Palestinian Legislative Council elections ending 40 years of Fatah-PLO leadership of the Palestinian people. Hamas vows never to recognize Israel and never to give up their claim to all of Palestine. And why would they? Israel is unilaterally withdrawing and conceding to their demands.

In the summer of 2006 the Second Lebanon War begins. Hezbollah terrorists, now the driving force in Lebanon, cross the blue line border and attack an Israeli patrol, killing 3 soldiers and capturing 2 more (Eldad Regev and Ehud Goldwasser). The Hezbollah begins a series of rocket attacks on northern Israel under the leadership of Hassan Nasrallah. Hezbollah, armed by Syria and funded by Iran, fires hundreds of rockets at Israeli cities in the north. In subsequent days, Israel carries out massive but selective bombing and artillery shelling of Lebanon, hitting rocket stores and the Hezbollah headquarters in the Dahya quarter of Beirut.

Prime Minister Ehud Olmert orders Israeli troops to avoid hitting any target which may result in the death of Arab civilians[16]. After not achieving any sustainable military victory for obvious reasons, Israel agrees to a cease-fire adhering to UN Security Council Resolution 1701. The UN subsequently provides cover for Hezbollah for a secure rearmament.

In Gaza, by now a Judenrien (no Jews allowed) area, Hamas begins a relentless barrage of rocket attacks against neighboring civilian communities in the Negev.

---

[16] Never before has any country in the history of the world endangered the lives of its soldiers to spare civilians who were giving cover to those attacking them.

Without a Jewish presence in the area, the rocket attacks become a daily activity for Hamas operatives[17]. In March 2007, a new "Palestinian unity government" is formed to include Hamas and Fatah in a coalition government, Peres declares that "only with economics can we make peace" and insists that Israel must concentrate in helping terrorists find ways to become economically successful. Furthermore, Peres refuses to comment on the war curriculum that Abbas and the PA ministry of education have introduced in the PA. Peres consistently refuses to say if he has even reviewed the new PA school books, which have introduced a curriculum of war for the next generation of Palestinian Arab school children. Terrorist attacks increase form Gaza, using even younger fighters, this in violation of the Geneva conventions. From December 2008 to January 2009 Operation Cast Lead is set up to stop Hamas rocket attacks. Over 1,000 Palestinian casualties bring the mission to a halt before the IDF reaches its objectives.[18]

On April 2009 Likud party head Benjamin 'Bibi' Netanyahu becomes Prime Minister once more, and it is probably due to a serious lack of alternatives. Ehud Olmert's corruption had come to light and he is out of the political arena for good. Tzipi Livni, the daughter of a Jewish fighter, heads the Kadima mutant party. Ehud Barak, Israel's most corrupt yet decorated General heads the Labor party and a surprisingly victorious Avigdor Lieberman, with the support of a large percentage of the Russian population of Israel, gains enough seats in the Knesset to guarantee himself a part of any coalition. Lieberman, known for his right-wing rhetoric vows to strip disloyal Israeli-Arabs from their citizenship if they show their support to Israel's enemies including the Palestinian Authority. Lieberman quickly backtracks from his promises and commitments, as most politicians frequently do.

---

[17] 80 rockets were fired daily until operation cast lead is placed in action
[18] Rocket attacks persist until this very day.

Prime Minister Netanyahu also proves his lack of loyalty (and backbone) to the Likud's original right-wing platform by nominating Ehud Barak as Defense Minster and allowing Shimon Peres to serve as President[19].

In the US a new president is elected in 2008: Barak Hussein Obama. A somewhat obscure African-American man with a Muslim name and ties to socialist and communist advocates. The US tacit allegiance to the Muslim Brotherhood becomes stronger than ever before. The US, Europe, Russia and the Arab world present Israel with a list of demands: They insist Israel must give up the lands it liberated in 1967; that they must cede the Golan Heights to terrorist-sponsoring Syria; that they must give up Judea and Samaria (the West Bank) and half of the city of Jerusalem to the very same Arabs who have pledged to destroy Israel. Moreover, Israel must then agree to a suicidal Law of Return so that millions of so-called Palestinians can come and join their comrades and destroy Israel from within. Ludicrous indeed; still, Netanyahu hesitates and then begins looking for ways to capitulate. The Jewish population in the West Bank grows, much against the will of the government. The Arab birth rate is slows down. The 10,000 Jews that were thrown from their homes in Gaza and northern Samaria, many who are still homeless and awaiting compensation, settle mostly in the Samarian hills and vow not be moved again. The mere thought of wanting to remove 350,000 Jews to appease an Arab enemy which has no intention of making any real commitment of peace becomes a daunting prospective for the political demagogues that surround the Prime Minister.

"..to give Arabs who strive for Israel's demise, political rights equal to those of Jews who struggle for Israel's welfare, is not consistent with justice."
PROFESSOR PAUL EIDELBERG

---

[19] The Presidency in Israel is more of a diplomatic position than a leadership role.

"The Oslo accords were a Trojan Horse; the strategic goal is the liberation of Palestine from the [Jordan] river to the [Mediterranean] sea"
Faysal Al-Husseini, Palestinian Authority Minister for Jerusalem Affairs, in his last interview, 'Al-Arabi' daily newspaper (Egypt), June 24, 2001

THE PRESENT

"In the land of Israel
anyone who doesn't believe in miracles
is not a realist."
David Ben Gurion

In 2013 Bibi Netanyahu wins the elections once more. Although surrounded by many right wing colleagues, he invites Tzipi Livni, a leftist advocate to join his coalition. He capitulates to Obama's call for a freeze in new building construction throughout Judea, Samaria and Jerusalem. Jews fear that he will soon begin attempts to expel settlers from their homes. But Israel's number one problem, besides the fact that Syria's weapons of mass destruction (chemical and biological warheads) could be used against the Jewish State, is Iran and the continuation of its nuclear program. It is estimated that Iran will have working nuclear ballistic missiles before year's end. Rockets continue to be fired from Gaza into Jewish communities in the south, and in Lebanon, the Hezbollah has been amassing a significant number of missiles that could inflict grave damage to all of Israel.

Adding to this distressful time is the fact that Barak Hussein Obama is reelected as President of the United States, assuring four more years of unfriendly relations between the two countries.

In 2013 the Muslim world experiences popular revolts termed by the world media as "the Arab spring". Bloody revolutions shake the political arena of the Middle East. Although the first revolt occurs in Tunisia in 2010 when the people overturned the dictatorship there, it continued throughout the entire Middle East. In Egypt, the 30 year rule of Hosni Mubarak comes to an end. Hundreds are officially reported killed in street protests. Egyptians through the Internet, especially using social sites report the numbers of protestors killed in the thousands. The Muslim Brotherhood takes control of the Egyptian government and all political and legislative institutions. Fringe groups consider the victory of

Islamists as a signal to go on a killing spree of Coptic Christians. Hundreds are murdered, the majority being women and children.

In Libya, their dictator Colonel Mu'ammar Gadaffi, who ruled since 1969 comes to an end. The revolutionaries murder the leader in his hometown of Sirte and establish an Islamist regime. In Yemen, President Abed al-Hadi is forced to step down. Protests become a common occurrence in Sudan. In Jordan, King Abdullah shuffles cabinet members to appease protesters while persecuting and systematically murdering leaders as they become known to his regime. Prime Minister Nasser Al-Sabah resigns his mandate in Kuwait. But nowhere is the Arab uprising met with such brutal force as in Syria. Bashar Al-Assad gives orders to execute and even massacre anyone associated with rebels and protestors. An armed militia is formed and a civil war erupts which is still ongoing. So far, 110,000 men, women and children have been massacred by the ruling force while close to 20,000 Syrian soldiers have been killed in retaliation. There is a deafening silence in the UN and other world organizations regarding these brutal killings.

No one can get Arabs to stop killing each other. No one is hopeful that they will make peace any time soon; even so, world powers expect them to make peace with Israel. And the way to accomplish this idyllic peace is by having Israel continue to make unilateral concessions to a people incapable of recognizing their right to exist.

CONCLUSION

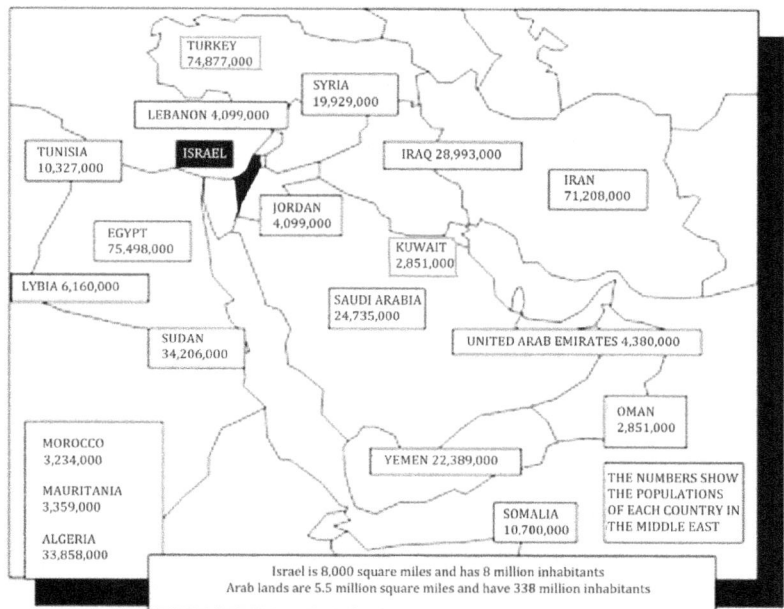

TURKEY 74,877,000

SYRIA 19,929,000

LEBANON 4,099,000

ISRAEL

TUNISIA 10,327,000

IRAQ 28,993,000

IRAN 71,208,000

JORDAN 4,099,000

EGYPT 75,498,000

KUWAIT 2,851,000

LYBIA 6,160,000

SAUDI ARABIA 24,735,000

SUDAN 34,206,000

UNITED ARAB EMIRATES 4,380,000

OMAN 2,851,000

MOROCCO 3,234,000

YEMEN 22,389,000

MAURITANIA 3,359,000

SOMALIA 10,700,000

THE NUMBERS SHOW THE POPULATIONS OF EACH COUNTRY IN THE MIDDLE EAST

ALGERIA 33,858,000

Israel is 8,000 square miles and has 8 million inhabitants
Arab lands are 5.5 million square miles and have 338 million inhabitants

(Figures on this map are based on World Almanac's publication of 2012)

On the eve of Rosh HaShana 5773 (September 2012) the total population of the State of Israel totals over 8 million residents (8,012,400), composed as follows: 75.4 percent (6,015,000) are Jewish; 20.6% (1,648,000) are Arab (both Muslim and Christian); and the remaining 4% (319,000) are either non-Arab Christians or people with no religious affiliation.

In the U.S.A., Jews number 5.3 million. In France, 485,000. In Canada, 375,000. In Great Britain, 292,000. In the Russian Republic, 205,000. In Argentina, 182,000. In Germany, 119,000. According to this data, 46% of world Jewry lives today in the State of Israel.

Israel is 640 times smaller than the Arab world, smaller than the State of New Jersey and roughly half the size of Lake Michigan. The combined size of the 21

Arab states is 5.3 million square miles, that's almost double the size of the United States!

Israel is only 1/6 of 1% of the landmass of the Middle East, and a large percentage of the Arab lands are uninhabited with soil is as varied as it was Israel's prior to Jewish immigration. The Arab-Israeli question cannot possibly be about the Arab need for more land, especially a corner that meant nothing to them for 1200 years. Rather, it is a religious conflict fueled by Arab hatred, intolerance and contempt. It is about an invented people with an invented political struggle where the victimizer is portrayed as the victim; and the only possible solution to this seemingly endless conflict, continues to be the transfer of the Arab population out of the disputed territories and the establishment of a strong Israel with secure borders. As for the so-called Palestinians, although these people have at best an historically void and pseudo-identity, they still need a place to call home. For all intends and purposes, Jordan has been and still is more of Palestine than Israel was or ever will be.

The subject of transfer is enormously complex. For starters, what will the two million Arab 'Palestinians' who live and depend on world charity do? Build a country as Jews did? Renounce terrorism? And there is the unquestionable fact that no one wants them, including Jordan. 'Palestinians' are considered the riffraff of the Arab world. The word Palestinian is used throughout the Middle East as a term to denote second class Arab workers at best.. Adding to the equation, can the Muslim world deal with a stronger and healthier Israel? Can

Islam come to terms with such a scenario? Being that no viable answers exist so far, transfer will continue to be considered an unrealistic option. Unfortunately, the alternative -meaning the perpetuating status quo- will only lead to more bloodshed for both peoples.

Not a day goes by, walking the streets of Israel, riding the buses and trains, looking at the fields, the skyline of the big cities, the promenades, the parks and the industrial centers that I don't hold my head in astonishment. I'm mesmerized by the country Jews have built from the sand, but for the life of me, I cannot understand their insecurities and myopic view of reality. Their mindset is that of a downtrodden people that have been kept in ghettos for so long, that feelings of freedom and victory are completely foreign. They have been oppressed for so long, they see their Palestinian counterparts as a reflection of who they have been for centuries, and have an uncontrollable urge to take their side, even at the expense of their own lives. The prophecy of Isaiah comes true before our very eyes, "*your enemies and your destroyers will come from within*". Through silence no good will come. Inaction will lead to our demise. Now more than ever, let the righteous stand, let the truth be boisterously heard!

> *"We will remember not the words of our enemies,*
> *but the silence of our friends."*
> MARTIN LUTHER KING, JR.

"The great enemy of the truth
is very often not the lie
-deliberate, contrived and dishonest-
but the myth
-persistent, persuasive and unrealistic-"
JOHN F. KENNEDY

IN OTHER WORDS

Larry Miller, a brilliant writer and comedian shares his insight as to what is the root cause of the Arab-Israeli problem in his article entitled:

<u>Whosoever Blesses Them, The intifada and its defenders</u>

A brief overview of the situation is always valuable, so as a service to all Americans who still don't get it, I now offer you the story of the Middle East in just a few paragraphs, which is all you really need. Don't thank me. I'm a giver.

Here we go: the Palestinians want their own country. There's just one thing about that: There are no Palestinians.

It's a made up word.

Israel was called Palestine for two thousand years. Like "Wiccan," "Palestinian" sounds ancient but is really a modern invention. Before the Israelis won the land in war, Gaza was owned by Egypt, and there were no "Palestinians" then, and the West Bank was owned by Jordan, and there were no "Palestinians" then. As soon as the Jews took over and started growing oranges as big as basketballs, what do you know, say hello to the "Palestinians," weeping for their deep bond with their lost "land" and "nation." So for the sake of honesty, let's not use the word "Palestinian" any more to describe these delightful folks, who dance for joy at our deaths until someone points out they're being taped. Instead, let's call them what they are: "Other Arabs From The Same General Area Who Are In Deep Denial About Never Being Able To Accomplish Anything In Life And Would Rather Wrap Themselves In The Seductive Melodrama Of Eternal Struggle And Death."

I know that's a bit unwieldy to expect to see on CNN. How about this, then: "Adjacent Jew-Haters."

Okay, so the Adjacent Jew-Haters want their own country. Oops, just one more thing. No, they don't. They could've had their own country any time in the last thirty years, especially two years ago at Camp David. But if you have your own country, you have to have traffic lights and garbage trucks and Chambers of Commerce, and, worse, you actually have to figure out some way to make a living. That's no fun.

No, they want what all the other Jew-Haters in the region want: Israel. They also want a big pile of dead Jews, of course-that's where the real fun is-but mostly they want Israel.

Why? For one thing, trying to destroy Israel-or "The Zionist Entity" as their textbooks call it-for the last fifty years has allowed the rulers of Arab countries to divert the attention of their own people away from the fact that they're the blue-ribbon most illiterate, poorest, and tribally backward on God's Earth, and if you've ever been around God's Earth, you know that's really saying something. It makes me roll my eyes every time one of our pundits waxes poetic about the great history and culture of the Muslim Mideast.

Unless I'm missing something, the Arabs haven't given anything to the world since Algebra, and, by the way, thanks a hell of a lot for that one.

Chew this around and spit it out: Five hundred million Arabs; five million Jews. Think of all the Arab countries as a football field, and Israel as a pack of matches sitting in the middle of it.

And now these same folks swear that if Israel gives them half of that pack of matches, everyone will be pals. Really? Wow, what neat news. Hey, but what about the string of wars to obliterate the tiny country and the constant din of rabid blood oaths to drive every Jew into the sea? Oh, that? We were just kidding.

My friend Kevin Rooney made a gorgeous point the other day: Just reverse the numbers. Imagine five hundred million Jews and five million Arabs.

I was stunned at the simple brilliance of it. Can anyone picture the Jews strapping belts of razor blades and dynamite to themselves? Of course not. Or marshalling every fiber and force at their disposal for generations to drive a tiny Arab state into the sea? Nonsense. Or dancing for joy at the murder of innocents? Impossible. Or spreading and believing horrible lies about the Arabs baking their bread with the blood of children? Disgusting. No, as you know, left to themselves in a world of peace, the worst Jews would ever do to people is debate them to death.

Mr. Bush, God bless him, is walking a tightrope. I understand that with vital operations coming up against Iraq and others, it's in our interest, as Americans, to try to stabilize our Arab allies as much as possible, and, after all, that can't be much harder than stabilizing a roomful of supermodels who've just had their drugs taken away. However, in any big-picture strategy, there's always a danger of losing moral weight. We've already lost some. After September 11 our president told us and the world he was going to root out all terrorists and the countries that supported them. Beautiful.

Then the Israelis, after months and months of having the equivalent of an Oklahoma City every week (and then every day) start to do the same thing we did, and we tell them to show restraint. If America were being attacked with an Oklahoma City every day, we would all very shortly be screaming for the administration to just be done with it and kill everything south of the Mediterranean and east of the Jordan. (Hey, wait a minute, that's actually not such a bad idea... uh, that is, what a horrible thought, yeah, horrible.)

DOWN WITH JABOTINSKY

The following speech was given in front of an American Audience a short while after Rabbi Kahane, a controversial political figure, received one seat in the Israeli Knesset (Parliament) in 1984[20]. Note that this speech was given before the Oslo Accords were signed and before the PLO (Palestinian Liberation Organization) received land and weapons and became the Palestinian Autonomy. It was before suicide-bombings and the Intifada (Arab uprising), and 15 years before 9-11.

Rabbi Kahane speaks:

'They hated him in the gates he who rebukes, and they abhorred he who speaks the truth" a verse from the book of Amos[21].

In 1938 Ze'ev Jabotinsky visited Vilna and the leftists in Vilna particularly the Socialist Bundt, put out a leaflet, which they handed out to the Jews of Vilna. I want to read it to you. Ze'ev Jabotinsky of course was the greatest of the Zionist leaders of his time and in 1938 he was appealing to the Jews of Poland and Europe to escape, to run, to leave before tragedy struck them. And the Bundt issued the following leaflet, which has been translated from Yiddish into English:

"To the Jewish workers and the Jewish masses of Vilna, the spiritual father of Jewish fascism, the paper general Jabotinsky is coming to Vilna. Of late this adventurer and charlatan has become very popular with the Jewish workers and Jewish masses of Vilna; show your contempt for the Purim general and give him this command: Get out! Evacuate yourself along with your friends from Poland. Down with Fascism, Down with Jabotinsky."

---

[20] Transcript recorded first hand by Ze'ev Shemer
[21] Amos was one of the Biblical prophets in the Tanach who forewarned the Jewish people of the upcoming Roman siege.

When I read this particular leaflet, it reminded me of the truth that nothing ever changes. Nothing ever changes! The Jewish people learn nothing from History, repeat the same tragedies. I cannot begin to tell you, the hate, the sheer psychopathic hate, which is raging today in the state of Israel. Not against Arafat and not against the PLO, and not against Syria but against Jews!

They have created a new label in Israel called "Kahanism", and I want you to know what Kahanism is, Kahanism is a label and an outlet for vicious hatred against Judaism. And those who march against Kahanism tomorrow will march to trample on Judaism.

In Givatayim, a suburb of Tel Aviv 10,000 leftists came from all over the country. Bused in from the Kibbutzim, they came with iron bars, they came with stones, they attacked Jews, they beat Jews. The Mayor of Givatayim, a member of the Marach (Labor party), stood and shouted "laarog otam kaasher hem ktanim!" - kill them while they are still small! This is the face of the left in Israel. And as I watched that crowd, the twisted faces, the obscenities, the curses, I said to myself, now I understand what happened in Israel 40 years ago, at the time of the "HaSidon" - The Season. And everyone must know what happened in those days.

It is those that don't know what happened in the past that will live to see it happen again in the present and in the future.

In the 1940's these same Kibbutznikim, HaShomer HaTzair, Meretz, Labor, the same liberal Jews that today speak about democracy, and love of all the people, they speak about ethics, and morality... they kidnapped Jewish soldiers of the Irgun and Sternist Jewish fighters, and they turned them over to the British, knowing that to be a member of the Irgun was a capital punishment, a death sentence.

They were the ones who in 1948 fired upon the Irgun ship, the Altalena (a ship that was smuggling weapons for the Jewish fighters to use against the British and

Arab militants) and murdered in cold blood 17 Jews because Menachem Begin was on the ship and they wanted to liquidate Begin. And know who the commander of the operation was, his name was Yitzhak Rabin. He gave the order to fire and to murder 17 Jews. And know that the next day in the Knesset, the Prime Minister at that time, Ben Gurion, rose and in the minutes he said, "blessed be the holy canon", blessed be the holy canon that murdered seventeen Jews!

They speak to us about Democracy and about love? They were the ones who murdered in cold blood in the 1920's one of the leaders of Agudat Israel, Yaakov Yisrael Dahan, because he was an anti-Zionist. So you can oppose an anti- Zionist, but to murder a Jew in cold blood? And know who gave the orders: Yitzhak Ben Zvi, the second President of the State of Israel. They speak about Fascism? About hooligans? They turn now to the Sephardic Jews and tell them to watch out for Kahane! They turn to Sephardic Jews? The leftists? How ironic, because I remember what they did! How they destroyed whole communities of Jews from Morocco, and Algeria and Libya, and Tunisia and Egypt, and Syria and Iraq and Yemen!

In the 1940's as the State came into being, hundreds of thousands of Jews poured in from Arab countries. Every one of those Jews was a Zionist, a real Zionist, not the Herzl type of Zionist! They were Zionists for 2000 years, "ve techezena enenu leTzion" - may our eyes behold the return to Zion. That was real Zionism. They were warm Jews, religious Jews, and what happened to them! The leftists from Mapai and Mapam stood and watched as 800,000 Jews poured into the country, and they asked themselves the only question that had any meaning to them, the only thing that bothered them, the thing that meant more to them than the State, than the Jewish people, the question was: "For whom will they vote?" They saw they were all religious Jews, "they will not vote for us" they thought, so they went about purposely in cold blood, to spiritually destroy an entire people.

Jews were put into 'mabarot,' transit camps, and if there was a job, they asked you "in what school have you registered your child?" and if it was a religious school, there was no job! And they would say, "take this paper and take it to the

92

Histadrut School (Labor Union), register your child in a Histadrut school; the Principal will then stamp the paper and you will bring it to the Labor Exchange office and you will get a job." If you wanted a job they would ask, "where is your red book of the Histadrut? You are not a member? No job!"

Fascism? I know who the Fascists were and who the Fascists are! The pity is that we waited 37 years to put someone in the Knesset to give to them, just as they gave to us! I have arrived!!

They speak of "kfiat dati" - religious coercion. Llet me speak to you about religious coercion. In 1948 10,000 Yemenite boys, children, came to Israel without their parents under the auspices of Youth Aliyah. Every Yemenite boy that came to Israel, came with his Shabbat, with his Kashrut, and with his "Simanim", that's what they called the "peyott" - the ear-locks that every Yemenite boy had. The Simanim, the sign of the Jew. For 2000 years they had the Simanim, for 2000 years they had the Shabbat, for 2000 years they suffered but remained Jewish, then they came to the Holy Land to places as 'holy' as the Kibbutzim of the Shomer HaTzair[22]. They ripped from them their Simanim, their Judaism, their Jewishness, children ages 7, 8 and 9.

Shimon Peres speaks today about the tragedy that there is crime in Israel. Crime in Israel? "Boker Tov" - good morning! If there is crime in Israel, who created it? If there are gangs in Israel, who created them? And if there is a breakdown in everything that is Jewish in Israel, who created that? If not Shimon Peres and his gangsters?! They ripped from Jews the only values they had, their Judaism, and left them naked to pick up the values of Dizengoff Street;[23] and now they complain about hoodlums and gangsters. I sat in prison in Israel; I saw the Yemenites, the Iraqis, and the Moroccans, who never knew what crime was when they lived in Morocco and Yemen and Iraq.

---

[22] Youth movement for the non-religious liberal new-Zionists.
[23] Dizengoff Street is in the heart of Tel Aviv, known for its nightlife, commerce and unfortunately an abundance of drugs and prostitution.

They never tasted it, they came to Israel and were destroyed spirituality by people who cynically cared only about "for whom will they vote?" So when I say these things in the 'Kikar' - in the town square, of course the people listen and of course people clap, and of course people cheer because finally someone is coming and saying the truth, he is saying what they have always thought all these years. You think it's an accident that so many people are shouting 'Kahane'? It's not an accident. I touched upon the things that bother them, that trouble them, the things that no one else is saying to them. I want a Jewish State. I don't want a Hebrew speaking copy of Time Square!

I want to give to those people, the Sephardic Jews that came to Israel with 'Kavod' - honor, self respect, the respect for the family, respect for their father, their mother, they came with respect and honor; and it was taken from them, and they were told, "your father is a 'primitivi' - a primitive; and your mother is a 'primitivit' - she is primitive, she is backwards". Backwards?

They who raised their children with honor and pride, to work and not to steal, they were primitive? It is the European, the Hellenism, this Western Hellenized culture, which first destroyed the Jews of the West and now they use it to wipe out the Jews from Arab countries. That will not be. I don't want a Hellenist State, I want a Jewish State and that is why they hate me so.

I want to save the Jewish soul and the Jewish body, and I want to tell you that the Jewish body is in danger every day in Israel. If I mention the name Motty Swuissa I don't know if 10 people here know the name. But Motty Swuissa just two weeks ago was murdered. He was murdered in Israel; not in Lebanon and not in the 'Occupied Territories ' of Yossi Sarid. He was murdered near Beit Shemesh, 20 kilometers from Yerushalayim he and his fiancé were murdered in cold blood by Arabs. The same day another Jew was murdered in the north, in Migdal HaEmek. This is a pattern now; they are killing Jews in Israel every single week. Who cares? What is the answer? We came to Israel to die? We came to Israel to live. Today for the first time Jews in Israel are frightened, Jews are afraid in Israel. It's becoming Brooklyn.

A Jewish woman comes to me in Kiriyat Atta, a suburb of Haifa, and tells me "I'm afraid to let my child play in the streets." This is the dream of Zion? For this we waited 2000 years? Soldiers are afraid.

Shaltiel Akiva, -there aren't five people here who remember that name- a 21 year-old soldier from the Yemenite town of Rosh Ayin, who spent eight months in Lebanon without a scratch, he came back safely. The night he returned he was murdered. And the father told me the story after the funeral the next day; he said the previous evening his son Shaltiel, phoned and said, I'm at the 'trempiada' - the hitch-hikers' stop - five kilometers away from Rosh Ayin. For those that don't know, Rosh Ayin is near Petach Tikvah in the heart of Israel. "I am five kilometers away from home please prepare supper for me" so they prepared supper for him and they waited 15 minutes, and half-an-hour, and an hour, they waited all night and he never arrived. The next day they brought his body. Shaltiel had been murdered by Arabs inside the State of Israel while hitching a ride!

Moshe Tamam, -that name virtually nobody remembers- was a 19 year-old soldier hitching a ride near Netanya. Arabs picked him up and gave him a ride. They found his body four days later. And know what they did to him so you know whom we are dealing with. They gouged out his eyes, and they cut off his sexual organs; and that is what we are dealing with. And of such people our Rabbis told us already, and the Humash[24] told us already, "Ishmael will be a wild man, his hand will be against everybody and everybody's hand will be against him." That's with whom we're dealing! This is the enemy. This is Ishmael.

My son came home from the army, he came from Miluim (reserve duty) and he showed me a letter, which was given to every soldier; a letter from the Israeli Defense Forces. "Let me see the letter, let me see pride I told him." Do you know what the letter said? It said, "Hayal -soldier- be careful when hitching rides". Soldier of Israel be careful on the roads of Israel, you might be killed by Arabs in

---

[24] The Torah or Jewish Bible also referred to as the Five Books of Moses.

Israel! What a tragedy, what a disgrace, what a Hilul HaShem! (Desecration of God's name). But according to liberals the enemy is Kahanism?

All of this doesn't bother the enemies of Kahanism, but it bothers me. That Jews who came after 2000 years in the exile, are assimilating inside Israel. When you visit Israel you are tourists, you don't see anything. You see the Wall, you see Masada, and the Plaza Hotel; you don't see the tragedy that occurs not far from the Plaza and on every town and every city.

The Arabs come into the towns, to meet Jewish girls. In the morning the Arab wakes up in his village and he is Ibrahim, he comes to Jerusalem or Netanya and suddenly his name is Avi, "Hello, my name is Avi." There are over 3500 Jewish women married to Arabs and over 10,000 Jewish women living with Arabs in Israel. In Beit Shemesh I'll never forget the Jew that came over to me, a man in his 50's and said to me, "Rav Kahane," he said, "I have two daughters and they are both married to Arabs. One lives in the Arab village of Taiba." and then he said, "When I lived in Morocco did I ever dream in my blackest nightmare, that my daughter would ever go out with an Arab? In Morocco? Never heard of such a thing! We came to the Holy Land and my daughters married Arabs!"

That doesn't bother anybody?

The President of Israel "hometz ben yain" - vinegar the son of wine, the son of the chief Rabbi, this Helenist goes to visit Nevey Shalom, a settlement founded by a Jew who converted to Christianity and is now a monk; a settlement where Jews and Arabs live together, and he says "ze keren ohr" - this is a ray of light. This is our President? This is our president!

On the beaches of Israel in the summer time, you see cars parked, most with license plates from Shechem, Jenin, Tulkarm, Hevron, Aza, what are they looking for? Sun and water? There is sun and water in Aza (Gaza) too. They are looking for Jewish women! The prostitutes in Israel are all Jewish, the pimps are mostly Arabs and we, we bare the shame, because this is not new, this has been going on for 30 years. When did you last hear the religious (political) parties in Israel, let alone the other parties, speak up about this? The irony, it would laughable; it would be a joke out of Chelm if it weren't so tragic.

The religious head of the Druze, Sheik Taari, appealed to the chief Rabbi of Haifa to come out and oppose intermarriage of Druze men with Jewish women. So when you saw in the paper that the chief Rabbi of Haifa came out... no! After 20 years he came out because the Druze asked him too.

In Haifa they have, a center called Beit HaGefen. It is funded by the city of Haifa with public funds. It is a center for assimilation, intermarriage and the destruction of Jewish values. Jewish women and Arab men, and it is always Jewish women because an Arab woman is not allowed to go out of her village, let alone to go out with a Jew. The Arab goes into Haifa and there's no problem, he isn't afraid; but let an Israeli Jew go into an Arab village any evening to look for an Arab woman, they'll slice him into little pieces. Who speaks of these things? Who talks of this? This tragedy that is taking place today in Israel?

And above all, the tragedy of the gradual and not so gradual birthrate of the Arabs in Israel. Because we are such foolish people and unwise, we pay them for each baby, each month a check from 'bituach leumi'-National Insurance. For one baby, one check, two babies, two checks; ten babies? Here, take a book of checks! Every month! You want a tourist site? I'll give you a tourist site no tour guide would ever take you to: On the twentieth of every month go to the main post office, in every major city and watch the hundreds of Arabs in line waiting to cash their checks. And count how many checks each one of them has. 10 checks, 15 checks, 18 checks, why not? The Galilee today has a majority of Arabs. Today! Not in twenty years, but today!

Jews are afraid at night to drive through Arab villages in the Galilee, so they are building access roads to go around so God forbid we shouldn't have to drive through them. Entire cities in Israel are becoming Arab. Jaffa is becoming Arab,

Ramle is becoming Arab, Lod, Akko, Nazareth Ilit built by the Israeli government to meet the Arab Nazareth is today 25% Arab.

Why? Arabs come with dollars, and they offer twice the price for the apartment in cash. And where does this money come from? It is PLO money and comes across Jordan; and it comes across freely and the government knows about it. They are quiet about it and they say, "It doesn't hurt anyone, the important thing is they are quiet, and after all it's a Democracy" (sic).

They are buying Jewish land and we are committing suicide. I however, am not ready to commit suicide in the name of Democracy. For 40 years we have been 'frayerim' – fools; but I am not a fool, I will not sit quietly. I don't hate Arabs. I love Jews! And I hate the enemies of the Jews, not because they are Arabs but because they are enemies! You think there is a single Arab living in Israel in a place that is called the Jewish State?

Liberals have immense contempt for the Arabs; they believe that they can buy them. "We'll raise their living standards and then they'll be good Arabs" Good Arabs? What contempt! They think that a good Arab is one that will agree to the Jews living in what he considers to be his Palestine.

You think there is one Arab who enjoys living in a State where there is a law of return that applies to Jews and not to non-Jews? You think there is one Arab who enjoys living in a State, which has a National Anthem: Hatikvah, with words that say, 'nefesh yehudi omia' - the soul of the Jew yearns? You can imagine how that sits with them. You think there is one Arab who enjoys living in a State whose Independence Day celebrates his defeat? You can't buy a person by giving him an indoor toilet. "You see, you had no toilet, now you have one." You can't come and say as the UJA says: "What do you want? We came and we turned the desert into a garden" Let me tell you what the Arab says: "Yes it's true, but it was my desert and now it's your garden." I respect the Arab, and that is why he has to go!

Because I know you can't buy him, you can't buy his national pride; know that he hates the Jews and that if we allowed them they would do to us what Arabs do to other Arabs today in Lebanon, and Syria, and Egypt. They would do to us what they did to us yesterday. Do you know what Arabs did to us in the 1920's and 1930's? Do you know what they did to us? When there was no Kahane, no Begin and no other 'fascists'? Do you know what they did to us when there was no State of Israel? What they did in Hevron and in Jaffa, and Yerushalaym? How they murdered over 500 Jews in cold blood?![25] They would do that to us if we let them, but I am not going to let them!

I want an exchange of populations. Beginning in 1948 we took in 800,000 Jews from Arab countries; that was phase one. Now I want phase two: We took Jews from Arab countries? Well now we'll give them Arabs from the
Jewish country!

I am ready to offer the Arabs that want to leave voluntarily compensation for their properties, which is more that what they did for the Jews they expelled from Morocco, from Egypt, from Iraq. Do you know how much money Jews in those countries left behind? Billions of dollars, and they were never compensated for it. And when we signed the treaty with Egypt we didn't even have the decency, the self-respect to demand compensation for the properties seized by Gamal Abdel Nasser from the Jews in Egypt. I am better than they; I will give compensation to the Arabs that are willing to leave. And those that are not willing to leave, I will throw out without monetary compensation!

This is racism? My God, this is saving ourselves, this is self-preservation! I don't hate the Arabs, I wish them well, elsewhere! I wish them the very best in any of their 22 countries. I have only one, it is mine and I am not going to lose it to either Bush or Begin. We can't continue in this way. We cannot continue as the country rapidly becomes more Arab, not in 40 years, not in 30, in 10 the Arabs will help the leftists become a majority in the Knesset, a coalition of Yossi Sarid,

---

[25] This is an historical reference to the massacre of Jews by Arabs in 1929 (18 years before the re-establishment of the Jewish State).

Shimon Peres, Mr. Shemtov and the Arabs, that will be the coalition if we don't do anything about this.

I am appalled by Jews who say, "This is what the Germans did to the Jews." Did the Jews of Germany ever say, "Germany is our country and the Germans stole it from us? And when we become the majority we will take it back and call it Israel?" That is not what they said. The Jews of Germany wanted nothing more than to be the best Germans that ever lived. The Arabs don't want to be Israelis.

Let everyone know that when we came out to oppose the Camp David Accords and peace treaty with Egypt, they said "Kahane doesn't want peace", I want peace, but I knew what kind of peace we would have with Egypt. Peace? Any country with a modicum of self-respect would have recalled their ambassador from Egypt. If Egypt had done to them what they did to us: murdered in cold blood seven Jews. I don't know if any of you know what the real story is, I am sure that it came here to you as "one crazy Arab shoots..." and every time an Arab shoots, he's crazy. So the story came as 'one crazy Arab soldier shot Jews and also wounded his own soldiers', well that's a lie!

Another Egyptian lie. A typical Arab lie.

He wasn't crazy, he was a member of the Muslim Brotherhood and other soldiers stood by and watched him shoot, and three of our seven soldiers did not die right away, they laid there bleeding, and the Egyptians refused to allow medical aid. And those three soldiers bled to death. And Mubarak said, "Why should a little incident upset our relationship?" A little incident? If I would have been Prime Minister I would have given him a little incident!

I am tired. I'm tired of going to funerals, I didn't come to Israel to go to funerals; I came to Israel for 'smachot' - happy occasions, joy, and happiness. There is a growing fear in Israel and you can tell by the hysteria, the hysterical obsession with Kahanism. President Herzog is obsessed with Kahane, he goes to bed every night with 'Kahane'. Shimon Peres says Kahane is the greatest danger to Israel, I would have imagined that Syria would be, but no.

The army radio station Galey Tzahal, devoted last week 18 hours, an entire day to Kahane, to attacks on Kahane the army radio station! An army that is supposed to be above politics, being crudely used by politicians and do you know why? Because they are terrified, because they know that as much as they are against Kahane, in the streets, the people of Israel are for Kahane!

It's not an accident that the Sephardic Jews in Israel are for Kahane, why? Because they did not learn about Arabs in a seminar at Hebrew University, they learned about Arabs because they lived under Arabs. So naturally when Kahane says what he says; they say "kol hakavod" - with all the honor, (meaning -you're absolutely right), because I say what they think. And the young people they are with us and that's what terrifies the Labor and the Likud. Yes the Likud. Pains me more than anything to have to tell you that the Likud has joined actively with the leftists in physically breaking up rallies of the Kach movement.

It's not to be believed, people who once had this thing done to them, and I remember how Menachem Begin in 1952 was prevented from speaking to the people in Afula. Leftist hoodlums broke up his rallies, and now they do the same? Do you know why? They are afraid of losing votes. They know that the people say that the Likud of today is not the Likud of yesterday. The Likud of Begin is not what it once was.

And we have to stop being idol worshipers. We do not worship idols. The Likud should be backed if it does for the people, if it doesn't we don't back it. With God's help in the next elections the latest poll in Israel shows 12 seats for us in the Knesset. And I tell you that is not true, not true! For everyone who is openly and willing to admit that he will vote Kach, there is another one who will do so quietly. I am not interested in Seats; I'm going for the whole ballgame!

I want a government of Kahane, Ariel Sharon and Raful and then you will see what we will do. Finally for those who ask: "how can you do it? How can you throw a million and a half Arabs?" I'll tell you how. Three years ago I served in the army; I was stationed near Ramallah, in Samaria, the West Bank, and the Arabs rioted in Ramallah so they sent me to put down the riots.

I want to tell you, not more than five minutes passed, and the whole town heard "Kahane is here!" there was absolute silence in that town, the riots stopped. It is imperative you understand what the name Kahane means to the Arabs. For them it is a monster, it is terror, they hear Kahane and they are terrified! And that is good because that is the only language they understand.

So how will we move out the Arabs? Think for a moment. Three years from now the Arab wakes up in the morning, turns on the radio and hears in the news that Kahane is the new Prime Minister of the State of Israel. Can you imagine what he will feel? How will I move them out? There will be no need. Half will leave by themselves, the other half, will beg me, "let us go" and because I'm big about it, I'll let them go.

My friends, Israel is at a crossroads right now. The All-Mighty gave us with His kindness, His Hessed - mercy, He gave us a Jewish State after 2000 years, but He is not going to give us a Jewish State without us working and suffering if we're not going to make the kind of State that He wants. I want Democracy for Jews but I don't want Democracy for Arabs because otherwise there won't be a Jewish State! And for those people that say "that is not nice" you answer this question: If you are such Democrats, are you willing to allow the Arabs, peacefully, quietly, democratically to sit every night and make love not war and allow them to be the majority, quietly and peacefully? You would be shocked and amazed to know how many Jews in Israel would answer 'yes' in Israel.

We have to create in Israel a Jewish State not a State for Jews, I am sick and tired to hear the 'sabras' - (Jews born in Israel) come and say to me "I am not a Jew, I am an Israeli", I don't want to hear that again ever! I want a Jewish State and I want the public schools of Israel to teach Judaism, I want Jewish youngsters to know what is *tefillin* and what is a holyday, maybe they won't want to keep it but at the very least, give them the choice of knowing what it is being and not being Jewish.

On Wednesday I presented a motion of 'no confidence' in the Knesset because of the policy of the Ministry of Education which enforced a curriculum of meetings between Arab students and Jewish students. Mixed summer camps, Jewish children staying in Arab villages for the weekend and Arab children in Jewish towns for the weekend.

I presented a vote of 'no confidence' to the other Ministers and asked them, will you vote for a Jewish education and a Jewish State or will you vote for the coalition and for your seats and the money? You know how they voted... they voted for the coalition. That is the tragedy. I can understand a secular and leftist party but I cannot understand a religious party sitting by and watching our youngsters being destroyed, for whatever narrow reasons they may have.

There will be an election and when Peres returns from his Washington trip he will be on a coalition course with the Likud. Peres is ready to make far reaching concessions to Jordan. When he praised King Hussein as a man who wants peace, one can only recall when we liberated the Old City and found out what they had done to every synagogue. They destroyed every synagogue. And what they had done in Har HaZeitim - Mount of Olives, to the tombstones: they used them to pave roads and as latrine seats. He wants peace... he wants many, many pieces of Israel. The government is going to fall. Shimon Peres has worked hard this past year, he's got the strength and the Likud has fallen badly, there is going to be an election and they will try to stop us from running, with God's help that won't be because we have many answers to their intentions, we will be running.

Just as I told the people in Israel the choice in the next elections is between Kahane and Arafat; that is what the next elections will be all about. Kach or the PLO that's the choice there is no other choice! I appeal to you, save Israel, save your brothers and sisters and save yourselves, because God forbid, I would not want to be in your shoes if there is no more Israel. I said I would end here but there is one more thing I want to tell you because it is vital. I believe that the State of Israel has to be the State for all the Jewish people and has to be the trustee of all the Jewish people. And I don't believe that there are boundaries that Israel cannot cross when Jews are in trouble.

And I want to tell you, that as anti-Semitism in this country (USA) grows, there will be a need for an Israel that will do things that you are not ready to do. And I want to tell you, that with God's help when I am Prime Minister, the State of Israel will never say that there are Israelis that are in trouble, we will always say that if there are Jews in trouble anywhere, our hand will reach out everywhere against those who hate Jews.

I will take your questions now."

Rabbi Meir Kahane was murdered November 5th, 1990
after giving a similar speech in a New York hotel
where he urged American Jews
to come home to Israel.

CONCERNING THE JEWS

By: Mark Twain – Harper's, September 1899

"If the statistics are right, the Jews constitute but one percent of the human race. It suggests a nebulous dim puff of stardust lost in the blaze of the Milky Way.

Properly the Jew ought hardly be heard of; but he is heard of, has always been heard of. He is as prominent on the planet as any other people, and his commercial importance is extravagantly out of proportion to the smallness of his bulk.

His contributions to the world's list of great names in literature, science, art, music, finance, medicine, and obtuse learning are also way out of proportion to the weakness of his numbers. He has made a marvelous fight in this world in all the ages, and has done it with his hands tied behind him. He could be vain of himself and be excused for it. The Egyptians, the Babylonians, and the Persians rose, filled the planet with sound and splendor, and faded to dream stuff and passed away.

The Greeks and the Romans followed and made a vast noise and they are gone. Other peoples have sprung up and held their torch high for a time. But it burned out, and they sit in twilight now, or have vanished.

The Jew saw them all. Beat them all, and is now what he always was, exhibiting no decadence, no infirmities of age, no weakening of his parts, no slowing of his energies, no dulling of his alert and aggressive mind. All things are mortal but the Jew. All other forces pass, but he remains.

JEWISH WEAKNESS

Rabbi Menachem Mendel Schneersohn 'The Rebbe'

Menachem Mendel Schneerson (April 5, 1902 – June 12, 1994), known as 'The Rebbe', was a prominent Hasidic rabbi who was the seventh and last rabbi of the Chabad Lubavitch movement. He was fifth in a direct paternal line to the third Chabad Lubavitch Rebbe, Rabbi Menachem Mendel Schneersohn.

In 1950, upon the death of his father-in-law, Rabbi Yosef Yitzchok Schneersohn, he assumed the leadership of Chabad Lubavitch. He led the movement until his death in 1994, greatly expanding its worldwide activities and founding a network of institutions (as of 2006, in 70 countries) to spread Torah Judaism among the Jewish people, with the stated goal of "Jewish unity".

These are his words concerning the land of Israel:

"The humiliating concessions made by Israel under the Camp David[26] accords are a direct result of Jewish weakness. Instead of basing our claim to the land on God's promise to His people, we prefer to rely on the goodwill and generosity of the non-Jew. Instead of being proud and firm in our identity, we adopt non-Jewish attitudes and quail and cower before the gentile nations".

"The signing of the Camp David accords by Israel is the most senseless folly imaginable. We have ceded our security — lands, oil, settlements and airfields — for nothing but a piece of paper that can be torn up at any time. The "peace" we thought to gain is a bitter illusion, and the only result is that now we are infinitely weaker and the enemy infinitely more powerful."

---

[26] A reference to Menachem Begin's relinquishing of the Sinai peninsula to Egypt. The first time Israel gave up territory in exchange for political concessions. It was also the first time Israel recognized a Palestinian entity.

RATIONALE

"It doesn't matter if he's a terrorist or a traditional Muslim. At the end of the day
a traditional Muslim is doing the will of a fanatic, fundamentalist, terrorist God.
I know this is harsh to say. Most governments avoid this subject.
They don't want to admit this is an ideological war."

Mosab Hassan Yousef[27].

College campuses across the world are swamped with pro-Palestinian students that spew their hatred for Israel. These 'activists' recruit passionate yet ignorant students to join their cause. They convince them that they both have a common enemy: the bankers that have destroyed the American economy and the Jewish lobby that perpetuates the suffering of the Palestinians. Jews are at fault. Jews are the cause of the world's troubles and they must be dealt with. These advocates of the 'Palestinian' cause promise that once this enemy is defeated, the world will be a better place; there will be no more hatred of America, no more terrorism, no more suicide bombings, and no more fanaticism. To this lunacy, illiterate students and pseudo-intellectual professors subscribe blindly, without tendering their outrageous claims to any type of validation, and without ever allowing for a fair and open debate on the issues. 'The world will be better off without Israel', and the sheeple follow the wicked.

White Christian Aryans not too long ago made similar promises in Europe. Millions of 'undesired people' were sent to gas chambers, slaughtered, shot, raped and tortured, then either buried in mass graves or burned in crematoria. A third of the Jewish people was exterminated as well as hundreds of thousands of gypsies, blacks, people with disabilities, Je-hova witnesses and thousands of political prisoners so that Europe could become.... 'a better place'. And did it? Is Europe better off today than it was when Jews were a major driving force of its culture and development?

---

[27] Mosab Hassan Yousef, son of Sheikh Hassan Yousef (founder and leader of the Palestinian terrorist group Hamas). Mosab converted to Christianity and was disowned by his family.

Europe opened its doors to Muslim immigrants as a way to bring in cheap labor. What they brought upon themselves was a ticking time-bomb. Muslim terrorism in Europe includes the 1985 El Descanso bombing in Madrid, the 1995 Paris Metro bombings, the March 11th, 2004 bombings of commuter trains in Madrid in which 191 people were killed, and the 2005 London bombings, which killed 52 commuters; and that was only the beginning. According to EU Terrorism Report, there were almost 500 acts of terrorism across the European Union in 2006. In Marseilles, France, hordes of Muslim youths rampaged through neighborhoods, attacking local French citizens and shops after a soccer match. There are on average, 26 assaults by Muslims on non-Muslims per day in Marseilles. While Muslims make up approximately 10% of the population of France, they constitute in excess of 70% of French prison inmates.

On May 22nd, 2013 a British soldier standing guard near his barracks in Woolwich, southeast London was attacked and beheaded by knife-wielding Muslims. Two days later a soldier in Stockholm was stabbed by Muslim insurgents. Jews have been targeted to the point that it has become dangerous to be openly identified as a Jew in the streets of most European nations. Violent riots have plagued most major cities across the vast majority of Western European nations. Whether they are protesting a cartoon that depicts Mohammad in a certain way, or a country wants to pass a law that contradicts their understanding of Sharia (Muslim law), the excuses to rape, pillage and assault are abundant. Today, close to a fifth of Europe's population is Muslim and their percentages are only getter stronger.

In universities across Europe and America we see the twisted faces of hundreds of students, sometimes accompanied by their teachers and professors, screaming, cursing, and venting their anger and hatred toward Jews. And they disguise their racism, neo-Nazism and bigotry by claiming they are only against Zionists! As if there is a difference! And the same bigots will jump at the opportunity to flash pictures of ultra-orthodox men hugging the likes of Ahmadinejad in Iran, or the late President Hugo Chavez in Venezuela, when in fact, 'Neturei-kartas[28]' are no more than a few dozen misfits. They will point to Jewish pseudo-intellectuals that don't miss a beat to agree with their bigotry; the likes of Noam Chomsky, Norman Finkelstein, Michael Lerner and a few others that are just as misguided and evil as the bigots that popularize them. Those that hate Zion and Zionism, hate Jews, and consequently hate Israel. And their hatred leads them to support Muslims who not-so-behind-their-back call them sons of pigs and apes.

Israel has friends. Not many unfortunately. Many Christian groups, namely evangelical congregations openly support Israel and oppose anti-semitism. Still, some Christians and many Catholics feel threatened by the existence of Israel and evidence that God still has relationship with a people who denied their messianic deity. And the Vatican sees this. And Muslims see this. It is that seemingly eternal relationship between God and the Jewish people that invalidates who they claim to be. It is the pact that exists between God and the Jewish people that says to the rest of the world, "you are only second in My eyes". So some Christians will cut their nose to spite their face. Instead of bonding with Israel against barbaric Muslims, they choose to propagate their message of hate, ignoring the fact that Muslims will turn on them as soon as the Jews are out of the picture.

Last but not least are the traditional anti-semites; many which claim not to have anything against Jews. They simply want to end the 'occupation and the oppression of the poor Palestinians'. "We don't hate Jews, we hate Zionists", they say; and some Jews for fear of being targeted by these bigots claim not to be Zionists. But nothing is more absurd! A Jew is connected to Zion or he ceases to be a Jew. Every Jew is a Zionist. And the hatred displayed by Muslims and liberals is nothing but colorful anti-Semitism. Envy, jealousy, and sheer irrational hatred of Zionists is nothing but hatred of Jews.

---

[28] Neturei-kartas area very small group of ultra-orthodox, anti-zionist misfits based mainly out of New York.

For any Jew, to live today in America, in France, in England, or anywhere but Israel is incomprehensible. It has become increasingly clear that the future of the Jewish people is in Israel. And although hundreds of thousands of Israelis were brought up to reject Judaism, many do end up returning to their roots. And there are hundreds of thousands of proud and strong Jews that fearlessly live exactly where the world doesn't want them. What better way to know that we live exactly where we are supposed to than when the world hates us for it?

"How vulnerable is pre-1967 Israel, which is dominated by Judea and Samaria topography, which is surrounded by a most violent, unstable, unpredictable and unreliable neighborhood, which has not experienced intra-Arab comprehensive peace or intra-Arab compliance with most agreements for the last 1,400 years, which has never tolerated wishful-thinking?" Yoram Ettinger, prominent political analyst and former Consul General of Israel.

So what is the solution? Everyone knows what the solution is, and it is not a pleasant one; it's a horrific one, but less horrific than the alternative! The solution is to expel Arab nationalists[29] out of the land of Israel and to help them relocate in Jordan, or in Egypt or anywhere -pick from any of the 22 Arab countries that surround Israel. This would save Arab and Jewish lives alike. It would mean an end to the conflict, something that many powers of the world do not seem to want. Seventy percent of the population of Jordan is composed of 'Palestinian' Arabs. In fact, since 1950, Jordan has had 7 Palestinian Prime Ministers. The Palestinian Arabs are not homeless!

"Palestine is Jordan and Jordan is Palestine; there is one people and one land, with one history and one and the same fate." Prince Hassan[30]

"It is common knowledge that Palestine is nothing but southern Syria." Ahmed Shuqeiri (later the chairman of the PLO, to the UN Security Council)

---

[29] Arabs that identify as Palestinians
[30] Prince Hassan, brother of the late King Hussein, addressing the Jordanian National Assembly, February 2, 1970

Israel is being asked to self-destruct by setting indefensible borders and allowing the arming of an entity that has sworn to destroy her. No other country on earth has been, or is being, asked to do anything even remotely similar. India will not grant political independence to eight million Sikhs despite the Sikh terror campaign which included the assassination of Prime Minister Indira Gandhi. Sri Lanka will not allow an independent state in the north for the Tamils, in spite of Tamil terrorism. Iran, Iraq, and Turkey will not grant the Kurds autonomy despite the ongoing revolts. The Flemish and the Walloons, ethnically different, are in a cultural struggle in Belgium but no one suggests dividing the country. Look at the Spanish and the Basques, the Rumanians and the Gypsies, etc. Only Israel is being asked to divide into two. Only Israel must give its enemies the means to destroy her.

There has never been a case of a nation winning a defensive war and then ceding territory to the vanquished. Only Israel is expected to put this absurdity into practice. No nation in the world would ever agree to such a thing. The United States never considered returning California and New Mexico to the Mexicans. England is still laying claim to the Falkland Islands off the coast of Argentina, thousands of miles away from Great Britain. Jews did not wage war against anyone to take their country back. Jews poured into Israel after 2000 years of exile and worked the swamplands and the deserts to be able to re-establish their homeland. But anti-Semitism knows no boundaries, no logic, and no justice ever applies to Jews. Current US President Barak Hussein Obama, asserts that Israel must concede and that soon enough the Arabs will recognize Israel's right to exist. As Caroline Glick, a writer for the Jerusalem Post so eloquently said:

"By introducing the demand that the Arabs recognize Israel as the Jewish state, our leaders are only making matters worse. In presenting this demand, our leaders are suggesting that the Arabs have the power to grant or deny that which is not theirs to give or take away. Israel has implemented its commitments and surrendered land to the PLO. The PLO has never abide by its commitment to moderate its behavior. To the contrary, the PLO's response to every agreement has been to escalate its political and terror war against Israel."

Obama and his advisers claim that peace talks will improve Israel's relations with the wider Arab world. But the last 17 years expose this claim as both inane and wrong.

Glick concludes: *"Israeli land surrenders in exchange for pieces of paper have not convinced the Arab League member states to accept Israel as a permanent state in the Middle East. They have convinced Israel's Arab neighbors that Israel is weak and getting weaker. This in turn has signaled to the wider Arab world that its best bet is to join forces with the likes of Hamas and fund and otherwise actively support the war against the Jewish state."*

Liberal Jews in Israel and worldwide were fast at condemning Rabbi Meir Kahane for demanding a systematic transfer of the hostile 'Palestinian' population into Jordan. Even though most Jews know deep in their hearts that he was driven by a profound love for his people and that his proposal would save lives in the long run. Nevertheless, they allowed the Israeli elite to demonize him and even declare his ideas as racist and illegal. There was no outrage. Virtually no opposition.

Rabbi Kahane stated clearly that until the Arabs recognize Jewish sovereignty and put an end to their violent fundamentalism, healthy relations will never be achieved. And how right he was. Professor Paul Eidelberg points out that Prime Minister Binyamin Netanyahu is anxious to resume negotiations with Holocaust denier Mahmoud Abbas, evidence that Netanyahu --who is rich in oratory but poor in deeds-- is a politician and not a statesman. Abbas, who is extolled by fools as "moderate" recently nominated as his successor a Muhammad Ghaneim, a man that referred to the 1993 Oslo Accords as being too 'moderate'.

"What about the so-called Palestinian Arabs? Now that Netanyahu has endorsed a Palestinian state, what will be with them? I do not believe that a Palestinian state bordering Israel will come into existence, and for two reasons. First, if Abbas or his successor recognizes Israel as a Jewish state, he will be assassinated, as is Anwar

Sadat. Second, a Palestinian state would entail the expulsion of 300,000 Jews from Judea and Samaria. This will not happen. But making Israel more Jewish will lead to a large emigration of Arabs west of the Jordan River." Professor Paul Eidelberg

What is needed to solve the Israeli-Palestinian conflict, says Professor Eidelberg, is not the establishment of a Palestinian state, but to transform the State of Israel into an authentic Jewish Republic. In an article published by Palestinian Media Watch on July 28th, 2009, called "Historic opportunity at Fatah Sixth General Conference", Itamar Marcus and Nan Jacques Zilberdik describe with superlative accuracy the current state of affairs and the real state of mind of our 'peace partners':

"On Aug. 4-5, 2009, the Fatah movement will convene its Sixth General Conference - the first such gathering in 20 years and the first since the 1993 signing of the Oslo Accords. This official gathering offers a historic and unique opportunity for Fatah, and for Mahmoud Abbas, Chairman of both Fatah and the Palestinian Authority, to officially and publicly eradicate four Fatah principles that are basic foundations of the conflict. This would demonstrate to the world and to Palestinians that the Palestinians have joined the peace process."

Well Fatah did not recognize Israel's right to exist. Fatah leaders emphasize that this ideology is current and not merely an oversight.

"It is not required of Hamas, or of Fatah, or of the Popular Front to recognize Israel." [Al-Arabiya TV [Dubai] and PATV Oct. 3, 2006] Mahmoud Abbas

"I want to say for the thousandth time, in my own name and in the name of all of my fellow members of the Fatah movement: We do not demand that the Hamas movement recognize Israel. On the contrary, we demand of the Hamas movement not to recognize Israel, because the Fatah movement does not recognize Israel, even today." [PA TV March 16, 2009] Muhammad Dahlan, senior Fatah MP

Fatah continues to use maps that don't acknowledge Israel's existence. President Barack Obama has condemned such maps as a threat to Israel's security.

"I will never compromise when it comes to Israel's security... Not when there are terrorist groups and political leaders committed to Israel's destruction. Not when there are maps across the Middle East that don't even acknowledge Israel's existence." [AIPAC Conference, June 4, 2008] Barak Hussein Obama

To the left is terrorist leader Mahmoud Abbas
Note that Palestine is all of Israel

Such a map also appears as an official Fatah symbol under guns and under the PLO flag. When this symbol is created it had only one meaning - that Fatah would destroy Israel through violence.

Fatah charter still calls for Israel's destruction.

Article 8:

"The Israeli existence in Palestine is a Zionist invasion with a colonial expansive base, and it is a natural ally to colonialism and international imperialism."

Article 19:

"Armed struggle is a strategy and not a tactic, and the Palestinian Arab People's armed revolution is a decisive factor in the liberation fight and in uprooting the

Zionist existence, and this struggle will not cease unless the Zionist state is demolished and Palestine is completely liberated."

Fatah continues to endorse violence and terror. In the words of its leader, Mahmoud Abbas:

"Now we are against armed conflict because we are unable. In the future stages, things may be different... I is honored to be the one to shoot the first bullet in 1965 [Fatah terror against Israel begin in 1965], and having taught resistance to many in this area and around the world, defining it and when it is beneficial and when it is not... we had the honor of leading the resistance. We taught everyone what resistance is, including the Hezbollah, who were trained in our camps [i.e. PLO camps in '60s and '70s]." [Al-Dustur (Jordan), Feb. 28, 2008]

"I lived with Chairman Yasser Arafat for years. Arafat would condemn [terror] operations by day while at night he would do honorable things. I don't want to say any more about this." [PATV (Fatah), July 22, 2009] Muhammad Dahlan

So you ask yourself, how can it be that Israelis continue to play this game? How could it be that Israeli leftists ignore all of this?

Professor and Middle East Analyst and commentator, Emanuel A. Winston, wrote about Jewish Historical Revisionists[31]:

"The dedicated Leftists often identify significantly with their enemies, not understanding that the intended victims will also be themselves. A case In point is when Labor is no longer in office and sensitive negotiations were being conducted by Bibi Netanyahu, representing (more or less) the government's security position. The Labor party Leftists were reportedly in deep secret contact with Arafat's team advising them how to overcome Netanyahu's negotiators. As is usual in Israel, no one is indicted and sent to prison for betraying one's country to her sworn enemies. I cannot help but wonder if, in their final action while in control of Israel's

---

[31] Article published in 1999. After the signing of the Olso Accords but before Arafat's demise.

government, they will recommend assimilation and conversion to other religions such as Islam or Christianity.

Will Jews ever shake off their feelings of inferiority somehow, believing their accusers and persecutors must be right? I don't think so, particularly if those of the Left lead us with pathology that can only be described as suicidal."

So many Jews remain silent, and so many have chosen to stand on the sidelines both in Israel and around the world. The situation today is reminiscent of the years preceding the Holocaust. Co-founder of Z-Street, Lori Lowenthal Marcus explains:

"A very few World War II Jews acted as catalysts for those who refused to be cowed. They adamantly, sometimes theatrically, demanded action to prevent the incineration of millions of Europeans Jews, along with millions of members of other minority and political groups. This band of warriors, led by Peter Bergson and Ben Hecht, staged marches, rallies and theater events. They refused to mimic the Jewish leaders who shrank from their moral duty to demand the US government face the irrefutable facts of the plans, and then the execution of those plans, to murder millions."

During a speech sponsored by the Hudson Institute on September 25, 2008, Geert Wilders, a member of Netherland's Parliament had this to say about the Arab-Israeli conflict:

"The war against Israel is not a war against Israel. It is a war against the West. It is jihad. Israel is simply receiving the blows that are meant for all of us. If there had been no Israel, Islamic imperialism would have found other venues to release its energy and its desire for conquest. Thanks to Israeli parents who send their children to the army and lay awake at night, parents in Europe and America can sleep well and dream, unaware of the dangers looming.

Many in Europe argue in favor of abandoning Israel in order to address the grievances of our Muslim minorities. But if Israel were, God forbid, to go down, it would not bring any solace to the West. It would not mean our Muslim minorities would all of a sudden change their behavior, and accept our values. On the contrary, the end of Israel would give enormous encouragement to the forces of Islam. They would, and rightly so, see the demise of Israel as proof that the West is weak, and doomed. The end of Israel would not mean the end of our problems with Islam, but only the beginning. It would mean the start of the final battle for world domination. If they can get Israel, they can get everything. Therefore, it is not that the West has a stake in Israel. It is Israel."

And we must not forget that many of Israel's enemies are part of a fifth column. Many liberal Israelis have empowered Jew-hating Arabs with Israeli citizenship to use Israel's own democratic process to propel its demise.

Arab members of Knesset function as a psychological fifth column, openly backing Israel's enemies. Not one Arab politician has taken a stance against Iran. When Ahmadinejad says he is preparing nuclear bombs to "wipe Israel off the map" not one word of condemnation can be heard from Arab members. As if Arabs were impervious to a nuclear holocaust. It is as if they prefer their own death as long as Israel ceases to exist. And these are the 'loyal Israeli citizens'; the ones that receive social security, unemployment benefits, medical care, public education and social assistance. The same ones that attend Jewish universities and work in Jewish cities and industrial centers, and nonetheless most are sympathetic to our enemies even at the expense of their own welfare.

"Any Arab that serves the Israeli army is a disgusting criminal. We reject all forms of national service on behalf of Israel, because we are part of the 'Palestinian' people." Abdel Malik Dahamshe, Israeli-Arab Knesset Member, July 1998

Israeli-Arab Knesset Member Azmi Bashara (a neo-Nazi who praises suicide bombers, supports the Hezbollah, calls for Israel's destruction, and supports the enemies of Israel in a time of war). After the killing of three Israeli soldiers, he called Hezbollah (Lebanon-based terror group that attacks civilians in Israel's northern cities) *"a brave organization that has taught Israel a lesson."*

On June 8, 2000, Bashara at a "victory convention" in the Israeli-Arab town of Um el Fahm, announced to a crowd of Arab listeners:

"The Hezbollah has won, and for the first time since 1967 we have tasted the sweet taste of victory. The Hezbollah should be proud of their achievement and of humiliating Israel."

Bashara is an Arafat collaborator who proudly calls himself a "Palestinian Patriot!" He's joined by Israeli-Arab Knesset member Ahmed Tibi who for decades was Arafat's official adviser; a character that never misses an opportunity to spew his hatred and contempt.

At the March 2007 "Jerusalem First" conference in Ramallah, Israeli-Arab MK Ibrahim Sarsur calls on Muslims and Arabs to focus on 'liberating' Jerusalem.

"Just as the Muslims liberated Jerusalem from the Crusaders, so we must believe that today, too, the liberation of Jerusalem is not an impossible mission."

MK Haneen Zoabi became infamous in Israel after she took part in the attempted illegal invasion aboard the Mavi Marmara, a 2010 Gaza flotilla sent from Turkey, where Israeli navy soldiers who boarded the ship in accordance with Israeli law were lynched and only miraculously escaped death. When Zoabi returned to Knesset after the event, legislators erupted as she was brought to address the floor. Outraged, Yisrael Beytenu MK Anastasia Michaeli attempted to prevent the speech indignant liberal MKs created pandemonium.

Zoabi, who makes no quandaries about her identification with Israel's enemies has made countless anti-Israel speeches as a member of the Israeli parliament.

December 2008 her speech was particularly enlightening: *"Eighty-five percent of the Palestinian population was expelled in 1948. Today we are the third generation after the earthquake, 1.2 million Israeli Arabs, 18% of the population of Israel, a racist state, which uses tools for their religious domination. This is the reality of the policy of apartheid, very invisibilized, the media acting as a propaganda tool to justify indiscriminate massacres against the population who are women, children or elderly. In advertising for the dominator, the Palestinians are 'terrorists'."*

It has been the lack of courage to stand up to Jew haters outside and inside of Israel that has given anti-Semites the entitlement for Israel bashing. To know what is true and what is fabrication is only part of the solution. In order to survive as a people and although it may have sounded a bit too radical when Rabbi Meir Kahane proposed it to the members of the Israeli Knesset, today there is a clear realization that the only way for a Jew to survive, in Israel or abroad, is by strengthening our Jewish roots through the learning and performance of Torah laws, and to fight tooth and nail against our adversaries, never allowing ourselves to cave to international pressures. Let us never forget that when Hitler was killing a third of our nation, the silence of the world was eerily deafening.

The Arab-Israeli conflict is more than just the battle between Judaism and Islam. It involves more than only Israel and the Muslim world. If Judaism prevails, then those who claim to be perfected offshoots of what the Jewish people were originally meant to be, but had miserably failed at attaining, will be left with nothing. Now, after 2,000 years of exile, this downtrodden people, have risen to levels of greatness never seen before. Israel is a leading country in technology, medicine, literacy, all proof that God still maintains a relationship with His children. There cannot be two 'chosen peoples', and that is why this conflict is the most intensely watched, cared for, involved and complex battle scene on planet earth.

"Three passions have governed my life: The longings for love, the search for knowledge, and unbearable pity for the suffering of [humankind].

Love brings ecstasy and relieves loneliness. In the union of love I have seen in a mystic miniature the prefiguring vision of the heavens that saints and poets have imagined. With equal passion I have sought knowledge. I have wished to understand the hearts of [people]. I have wished to know why the stars shine.

Love and knowledge led upwards to the heavens, but always pity brought me back to earth; Cries of pain reverberated in my heart of children in famine, of victims tortured and of old people left helpless. I long to alleviate the evil, but I cannot, and I too suffer.

This has been my life; I found it worth living."
Bertrand Russell (1872 - 1970)

EPILOGUE

While doing a bit of research I stumbled upon an amusing site in the Internet, Jewlicious.com There is a posting by a user who goes by 'sarke' in which she is responding to Helen Thomas's anti-Semitic rant. Helen Thomas is a veteran White House correspondent who said on an interview *"Jews should get the hell out of Palestine".*

This was sarke's response:

"But let's be honest: the international community's human rights crusades on behalf of the Palestinians are just the latest Crusades, and the ones who REALLY suffer are not the Jews or the Israelis but the poor occupants of the Third World who are ignored while the enlightened First World castigates the Jews... and yes, of course, the Palestinians, who are kept in misery 'by their own leadership' in order to provide the polite Jew haters with a media club to beat them with.

So here's the thing: We are not going anywhere this time, Helen. We totally get it: Ya'll pretty much hate us. It's just the way it is, like a natural law. Nothing we can do - not giving away pieces of Israel (witness our evacuation of Gaza in 2005, and handing over the keys to army bases and greenhouses- a new economy! Food for the children! - which were summarily torched as property of the infidels); not donating billions annually to global charity, nor discovering a cure for Polio or the Theory of Relativity, or writing revered legal and religious texts, or co-founding Google, or manufacturing the microprocessor in the majority of laptops that spew Jew hatred to the Internet, or founding Christianity itself, or championing women's rights and gay rights in the US and helping to bring about a 'human rights revolution' in America in the 60ts, ...None of those things will absolve us of our real sin: Existing and overcoming.

I'm really sorry they told you to get the hell out of the White House, Helen. It really isn't your fault that you thought you could say what you said. It's not like it's a secret: That's what people think.

But this time, seriously. Getting the hell out is not in the cards. We're just sick of moving all the time.

I know. Irritating."

History for now, until it becomes one day re-written or 'revised', presents clear facts, proof of Israel's right to exist. One day we will possibly see history books which will omit the Holocaust or seriously minimize it. It will show that the Syrian-Greeks called the Philistines were the ancestors of the Palestinians of today. That there were millions of Arabs in Israel before the Jews arrived from Russia and Poland to steal their land. And that the Jews tried to delegitimize a people born to Biblical Abraham out of racism and bigotry. Lies will be built one on top of another which is why I felt it necessary to write this testimony to the truth of my days. Even as I speak, hundreds of thousands of pseudo-intellectuals are re-writing the Wikipedia files, Arabizing the Golan, the West Bank, Jerusalem and the rest of the Biblical land of Israel. Even the Bible and holy texts are being brought to question, ignoring the fact that the Bible precedes the Qur'an by 2,000 years!

My Muslim students asked to be excused due the celebration of a Muslim holiday. They told me it was the yearly commemoration of the "kurban" – the sacrifice. I was flabbergasted when they told me that Muslims commemorate yearly when Abraham (Ibrahim) took his son Ishmael and offered him as a sacrifice to Allah, only to have Allah stop him and ask him for a ram in his stead. The actual biblical story happens with Abraham's son Isaac, and not the son of his concubine Hagar. The Biblical story of Abraham and Isaac, completely rewritten for the Muslim faithful. They rewrite history, religion and even facts on the ground. There is a reason why Muslims during the past 1,500 years every time they conquer a city, the first thing they do is destroy the churches and synagogues and build mosques on the very same places others considered holy. Truth is not relevant to them. Islam means submission and they will do whatever it takes to become the dominant force. It may be only a matter of time before all lines become blurred.

If we fail to understand the truth, we fall prey once more to a long and overused routine of the world charging against the Jewish people.

Jews were accused of rejecting Jesus as the Messiah and savior of all humankind. Then, they rejected Paul and the New Testament. Centuries later Jews were accused of rejecting Mohammed as God's chosen Prophet, and today we are accused of occupying a foreign land and denying the Palestinian people their homeland. In between these major accusations Jews have been also blamed for the advent of Communism, of plotting to take over the world, and of killing Christian children and using their blood to bake *matza* (unleavened bread). Jews in Israel have been accused of harvesting organs of 'Palestinians', poisoning the water wells (never mind they're the same ones Jews drink from), of committing genocide, of giving radioactive toys to Arab children, etc. The voices of Jew-haters and anti-Semites that reverberate across the world know no limits. Jews are the communists, the capitalists, the fascists, they control the banks, they cause earthquakes and tsunamis, and if anyone is poor or has ever suffered any injustice, he can certainly trace the cause of his or her misery back to the Jews who are sure to be at fault.

Adding insult to injury, Holocaust denial is a thriving academic career that has found open doors in most universities worldwide. Scholars find no problem in denying the thousands of testimonials of Holocaust survivors who recorded in detail the atrocities committed by the Nazis, but also the thousands of accounts of American and Russian soldiers that discovered and liberated the concentration and death camps all over Eastern Europe. They have no problem in denying the thousands of pictures, film-reels, and documents -mostly recorded by the Germans themselves. With help of unJews such as professor Neve Gordon of Ben Gurion University, Norm Finkelstein, Noam Chompsky, the Holocaust will be questioned. The museums will be accused of fabricating facts. My dad who passed away in 2012 was probably one of the last to have survived the labor camps of Europe. Our testimony will be challenged.

Charging against Jews knows no limits because the motives of the masses are fundamental. They hate the message -there is a God in Heaven and we are accountable for our actions. Therefore, they must kill the messenger.

It is upon each and every one of us to know the history of the Jewish people, to know where we came from and to understand the historic significance of our being here. We must understand the significance of being Jewish.

It is possible that if you openly take on a pro-Jewish stance, you will be accused of being intolerant, of being a racist, or a fascist. You will be accused of being an extremist who is not giving Arab moderates a chance. It is you, they will say, who is not giving peace a chance. But know well, that there are no Arab moderates. An Arab that says he is fine with you not being a Muslim is himself a bad Muslim. He may be a good person but certainly not a true Muslim. Do not succumb to their pressure. As Stella Paul said in the September 2009 issue of American Thinker:

"And we're not going to chirpily 'dialogue' with professional Jew-haters who enjoy momentarily posing as 'moderate Muslims' to gain your puppy dog trust – and who then turn around and call us 'sons of monkeys and pigs.'"

Know well what they stand for, what they want, and the destruction they wish upon us.

Despite plenty of historical and archeological evidence that proves Israel's historic roots and disproves every Arab claim, most public and academic outlets will continue to profess that Israel's situation is a simple case of occupation of a foreign land. Ironically, they are right. There is an unfair and unnecessary occupation of land but not by the Jews that returned to their homeland, but on the part of the Arab multitude who assumed a fake identity with the sole purpose of destroying the Jewish dream of the rebirth of Israel; hence, the Palestinian nightmare.

Here in Israel, Rabbi Nahman Kahane explains, one finds thousands of batay-Knesset (synagogues), hundreds of yeshivot (learning centers) with tens of thousands of students and hundreds of thousand of people, men and women, who study Torah daily. Unprecedented in Jewish history of the last 2000 years and more. And although Israel is the 100th smallest country in the world, with less than 1/1000th of the world's population, our accomplishments are far and beyond our numbers. To not live in Israel is to choose to not be a part of the most important historical moment of our nation.

I live in the Galilee with my wife and children. We left a nice Jewish community in Hollywood, Florida. We left behind the shopping malls, the country club, a hi-tech job, a huge two-story house with a swimming pool and a Jacuzzi, two luxury cars, the maid, the driver and the gardener. Now, we live in a small but cozy home. I open my window in the morning and I see the Mediterranean sea. I drive to work and see sheep, I see cows, horses and roosters. It gets cold and muddy in the winter, but the air and the water are fresher and cooler than Florida will ever be. My kids ride their bikes to school, and even our dog seems to feel right at home.

Jews lived in the Golan, in the Galilee, in the West Bank and, yes, in Gaza since their return from Egyptian slavery 3,500 years ago. The Romans expelled most of our ancestors 2,000 years ago, but small enclaves always held on to the land, hoping their brethren would one day return from that lonely exile.

Well, some of us did return, and soon will most of the slumbering Jews who are for now, wrapped up in choices that prevent them from taking part in this most amazing ingathering. Although Israel is the size of New Jersey and thousands upon thousands of empty acres of land lay barren in the Arab world, it is this small corner in which surviving skeletons from both Europe and the hostile Arab world brought back to life; it is precisely this corner our accusers want, and now claim was theirs from the beginning.

These past 2,000 years have been tough. We witnessed the birth of Christianity and six hundred years later, the birth of Islam. With the exception of Hinduism, planet earth turned either monotheist or atheist, but much less idolatrous than it is when the Romans were burning our Temple down. A vast list of atrocities was committed against the Jewish people, and four all-out wars were launched against our young reborn country.

Now, terrorism is a common occurrence. Just this month, Arab terrorists in a drive-by shooting killed two teenage boys. That Jewish children can be shot and killed while waiting at a bus stop, that two boys could be killed simply because they are Jews, is something reminiscent of Nazi Germany. In whose eyes are Arabs justified in shooting unarmed teenagers in the middle of the street? Is this what an armed struggle is all about? Who can, as a Jew, support their cause and methods? And did anyone hear any condemnation by the UN? By European nations? By America? Did the news make page one? Of course it didn't! It may have been printed somewhere in page 14 under a headline like 'Two young settlers were killed by militants" or in the New York Times you'd probably read something more in the line with "Palestinians were afraid to go work today because Jewish extremists are protesting the gunning down of two settlers by a fringe militant faction."

Arabs are always innocent in the eyes of those who seek to delegitimize Israel. Terrorists became victims while victims became extremists. Israel must be hated to facilitate its destruction. UnJews want to be free from the obligations and restrictions of a true Jewish life. UnJews want to be free to eat what they please, to do as they please, whether it be on the Sabbath or on any other day of the week. Freedom to live a Hedonist lifestyle, pursuing physical pleasures. Freedom to chose right from wrong not according to God or to the understanding of a rabbinic court, but according to their own desires, to MTV, to Hollywood, to the immoral, and to the insane.

When will every Jew understand that this conflict is not about land, oppression or occupation? That Hitler did not hate the Jews because he is an Aryan and a racist –he allied Germany with Italians and Japanese! How Aryan are they? The Nazis and the Arabs both use excuses to justify their actions, but they also share the same base reason for their hatred of the Jews: they hate us simply because we are Jewish. Shimon Peres, Bibi Netanyahu, Ehud Barak and the other little ministers won't prevent more teenagers from being killed; yet, they can sleep at night because they know that they have many of you fooled. They will drag Jews out of their homes, free more Arab terrorists from jail; get a nice US dollar paycheck, a pat-in-the-back from the American President. All while Iran, unchallenged, builds nuclear bombs.

The time has come to bring a durable peace to this land; and instead of creating a pseudo-military force and financing hate-education and terror cells, we extend to all the Israel-hating Arabs our invitation to leave and live in peace. Arabs who wish to stay and accept Israel's Jewish character, are of course as they have always been, welcome.

There are twenty-two Arab countries, with land thousands of times larger than the entire tiny Jewish state; most of it empty and barren like Israel was before the Jews returned. The so-called Palestinians can settle there, live peacefully and prosper anywhere they choose. I know there are forces out there that are using these peasant Arabs as pawns in their sick political games. I know there are powerful people who want to see the situation deteriorate. But I would like to sit on my porch and read a newspaper where all the news is as nice as the view. I want the air that I breathe to be clean of conspiracies and men of evil. It is time for people of good to do what is right. It is time for the world to step back and let us pick our fruits in peace.

Maybe then, my brothers and sisters, those who sleep wondering if they should come, can feel better about taking the steps we already did. It is up to us now. The fate of Israel, the fate of the Jewish people, it all comes down to what we choose to do with the knowledge we acquire. Do we allow those that seek to do harm and re-write history to achieve their political goals? Do we sit back while evil and ignorance run amok and do away with what is good and right? Or do we stand firm and defend our homeland without fearing what friends or foes will say? We have waited for 2,000 years to come back home. Besides...

"We Jews have a secret weapon in our struggle with the Arabs;
we have no place to go."
GOLDA MEIR

DEAR WORLD

By Rabbi Meir Kahane
November 1988

Dear World,

It appears that you are hard to please. I understand that you are upset over us, here in Israel. Indeed, it appears that you are quite upset, even angry and outraged! Indeed, every few years you seem to become upset over us. Today, it is the brutal repression of the Palestinians. Yesterday, it was Lebanon; before that it was the bombing of the nuclear reactor in Baghdad and the Yom Kippur War campaign.

It appears that Jews, who triumph and who, therefore, live, upset you most extraordinarily. Of course, dear world, long before there was an Israel, we, the Jewish people - upset you.

We upset a German people who elected a Hitler and we upset an Austrian people who cheered his entry into Vienna and we upset a whole slew of Slavic nations - Poles, Slovaks, Lithuanians, Ukrainians, Russians, Hungarians, Rumanians. And we go back a long, long way in the history of world upset.

We upset the Cossacks of Chmielnicki who massacred tens of thousands of us in 1648-49; we upset the Crusaders who, on their way to liberate the Holy Land, were so upset at Jews that they slaughtered untold numbers of us. We upset, for centuries, a Roman Catholic Church that did its best to define our relationship through Inquisitions. And we upset the archenemy of the Church, Martin Luther, who, in his call to burn the synagogues and the Jews within them, showed an admirable Christian ecumenical spirit.

It is because we became so upset over upsetting you, dear world, that we decided to leave you - in a manner of speaking - and establish a Jewish State. The reasoning is that living in close contact with you, as resident-strangers in the various countries that comprise you, we upset you, irritate you, disturb you.

What better notion, then, than to leave you and thus love you - and have you love us? And so we decided to come home - to the same homeland from which we were driven out 1,900 years earlier by a Roman world that, apparently, we also upset.

Alas, dear world, it appears that you are hard to please. Having left you and your Pogroms and Inquisitions and Crusades and Holocausts, having taken our leave of the general world to live alone in our own little state - we continue to upset you.

You are upset that we repress the poor Palestinians. You are deeply angered over the fact that we do not give up the lands of 1967, which are clearly the obstacle to peace in the Middle East.

Moscow is upset and Washington is upset.

The Arabs are upset and the gentle Egyptian moderates are upset.

Well, dear world, consider the reaction of a normal Jew from Israel. In 1920, 1921 and 1929, there were no territories of 1967 to impede peace between Jews and Arabs.

Indeed, there was no Jewish State to upset anybody. Nevertheless, the same oppressed and repressed Palestinians slaughtered hundreds of Jews in Jerusalem, Jaffa, Safed and Hebron. Indeed, 67 Jews were slaughtered one day in Hebron - in 1929.

Dear World, why did the Arabs - the Palestinians – massacre 67 Jews in one day in 1929? Could it have been their anger over Israeli aggression in 1967? And why were 510 Jewish men, women and children slaughtered in Arab riots in 1936-39? Was it because of Arab upset over 1967?

And when you, World, proposed a U.N. Partition Plan in 1947 that would have created a Palestinian State alongside a tiny Israel and the Arabs cried and went to war and killed 6,000 Jews - was that upset stomach caused by the aggression of 1967? And, by the way, dear world, why did we not hear your cry of upset then?

The poor Palestinians who today kill Jews with explosives and firebombs and stones are part of the same people who - when they had all the territories they now demand be given them for their state - attempted to drive the Jewish State into the sea. The same twisted faces, the same hate, the same cry of "idbah-al-yahud" - "Slaughter the Jews!" that we hear and see today, were seen and heard then. The same people, the same dream - destroy Israel. What they failed to do yesterday, they dream of today - but we should not "repress" them.

Dear World, you stood by the Holocaust and you stood by in 1948 as seven states launched a war that the Arab League proudly compared to the Mongol massacres.

You stood by in 1967 as Nasser, wildly cheered by wild mobs in every Arab capital in the world, vowed to drive the Jews into the sea. And you would stand by tomorrow if Israel were facing extinction. And since we know that the Arab-Palestinians daily dream of that extinction, we will do everything possible to remain alive in our own land. If that bothers you, dear world, well - think of how many times in the past you bothered us. In any event, dear world, if you are bothered by us, here is one Jew in Israel who could not care less.

Rabbi Kahane left a strong legacy behind: a following of thousands of Jews who understand that there is an authentic Jewish Idea. That Judaism is not simply a religion or a ritualistic cult but rather, a way of life. That we should all strive to resemble King David: the Scholar-Warrior. Then we can proudly lift our heads and proclaim:

"I am a Jew!"

"Both Judaism and liberal, democratic western thought agree that the individual,
in order to protect himself, may disregard a government that refuses
to protect him, and that worse, prevents him from saving himself"
RABBI MEIR KAHANE ZT"L

LETTER FROM DOV

Dov Gruner is one of many valiant Jews who gave his life for the sake of the Jewish people. I leave you the following: The following letter from Dov Gruner to Irgun leader Menachem Begin is written before the British hanged Dov on the gallows .

(Translated from Hebrew)
April 16, 1947

Sir, From the bottom of my heart I thank you for the encouragement which you have given me during these fateful days. Be assured that whatever happens I shall not forget the principles of pride, generosity and firmness. I shall know how to uphold my honor, the honor of a Jewish soldier and fighter. I could have written in high-sounding phrases something like the old Roman *'Duce est pro patria mori'*, but words are cheap, and skeptics can say 'After all, he had no choice.' And they might even be right.

Of course I want to live: who does not? But what pains me, now that the end is so near, is mainly the awareness that I have not succeeded in achieving enough. I too could have said: "Let the future take care of the future.' and meanwhile enjoy life and be contented with the job I is promised on my demobilization.

I could even have left the country altogether for a safer life in America, but this would not have satisfied me either as a Jew or as a Zionist. There are many schools of thought as to how a Jew should choose his way of life. One way is that of the assimilationists who have renounced their Jewishness. There is also another way, the way of those who call themselves 'Zionists' - the way of negotiation and compromise, as if the existence of a nation were but another transaction.

They are not prepared to make any sacrifice, and therefore they have to make concessions and accept compromised. Perhaps this is a means of delaying the end but, in the final analysis, it leads to the ghetto. And let us not forget this: In the ghetto of Warsaw alone, too, there were five hundred thousand Jews. The only way that seems, to my mind, to be right, is the way of the Irgun Zvai Leumi, the way of courage and daring without renouncing a single inch of our homeland.

When political negations prove futile, one must be prepared to fight for our homeland and our freedom. Without them the very existence of out nation is jeopardized, so fight we must with all possible means. This is the only way left to our people in their hour of decision: to stand on our rights, to be ready to fight, even if for some of us this way leads to the gallows. For it is a law of history that only with blood shall a country be redeemed. I am writing this while awaiting the hangman. This is not a moment at which I can lie, and I swear that if I had to begin my life anew I would have chosen the same way, regardless of the consequences for myself.

Your faithful soldier,
Dov

"In a time of universal deceit, telling the truth is a revolutionary act."
GEORGE ORWELL

APPENDIX

Dr. Peter Hammond wrote a book entitled: *Slavery, Terrorism and Islam: The Historical Roots and Contemporary Threat.* I took the liberty to use some of the data presented and adapted its content for the purpose of presenting an appendix that hopefully will clarify the reasons I believe, impede a real and lasting peace with the Muslim world.

Hammond correctly points out that that Islam is not a religion, nor is it a cult. In its fullest form, it is a complete and all-encompassing system of life. Islam has religious, legal, political, economic, social, and military components. Muslims use Jihad, the struggle for Islam's global ascendancy, to annex and destroy worship places in order to validate their mythical religious beliefs. Their historical revisionism uses ideology, policy and strategy to completely negate the connection between the original people and their previous homeland. They have destroyed and covered over the histories of Zoroastrians, Buddhists, Hindus, and Coptic Christians; and they would gladly erase Judaism if they could.

Islamization begins when there are sufficient Muslims in a country to agitate for their religious privileges. When politically correct, tolerant, and culturally diverse societies agree to Muslim demands, some of the other components begin to creep into the fabric of their host society.

Here's how it works:

As long as the Muslim population remains around or under 2% in any given country, they will be for the most part regarded as a peace-loving minority, and not considered as a threat to other citizens. This is the case in:

United States -- Muslim 0.6%	Australia -- Muslim 1.5%
Canada -- Muslim 1.9%	China -- Muslim 1.8%
Italy -- Muslim 1.5%	Norway -- Muslim 1.8%

At 2% to 5%, they begin to proselytize from other ethnic minorities and disaffected groups, often with major recruiting from prisons, detention centers and among street gangs. This is happening in:

Denmark -- Muslim 2%   Germany -- Muslim 3.7%

United Kingdom -- Muslim 2.7%   Spain -- Muslim 4%

Thailand -- Muslim 4.6%

From 5% on, they exercise an inordinate influence in proportion to their percentage of the population. For example, they will push for the introduction of *halal food* (clean by Islamic standards), thereby securing food preparation jobs for Muslims. They will increase pressure on supermarket chains to feature *halal* on their shelves - along with threats for failure to comply. This is occurring in:

France -- Muslim 8%   Philippines -- Muslim 5%

Sweden -- Muslim 5%   Switzerland -- Muslim 4.3%

The Netherlands -- Muslim 5.5%   Trinidad & Tobago -- Muslim 5.8%

At this point, they will work to get the ruling government to allow them to rule themselves (within their ghettos) under Sharia -Islamic Law[32].

When Muslims reach or surpass 10% of the population, they tend to increase lawlessness as a means of complaint about their conditions. In Paris , we are already seeing car-burnings. Any anti-Muslim expression, whether perceived or imagined, results in uprisings and threats. Such tensions are seen regularly in places such as:

Guyana -- Muslim 10%   India -- Muslim 13.4%

Israel -- Muslim 16%   Kenya -- Muslim 10%

Russia -- Muslim 15%

---

[32] The ultimate goal of Islamists is to establish a global system of Sharia law.

After reaching 20%, of the population, nations can expect hair-trigger rioting, jihad militia formations, sporadic killings, and the burning of Christian churches and Jewish synagogues, such as in:

Ethiopia -- Muslim 32.8%

At 40%, nations experience widespread massacres, chronic terror attacks, and ongoing militia warfare, such as in:

Bosnia -- Muslim 40%   Chad -- Muslim 53.1%
Lebanon -- Muslim 59.7%

From 60%, nations experience unfettered persecution of non-believers of all other religions (including non-conforming Muslims), sporadic ethnic cleansing (genocide), use of Sharia Law as a weapon, and Jizya -the tax placed on infidels, such as in:

Albania -- Muslim 70%   Malaysia -- Muslim 60.4%
Qatar -- Muslim 77.5%   Sudan -- Muslim 70%

Beyond 80%, expect daily intimidation and violent jihad, some State-run ethnic cleansing, and even some genocide, as these nations drive out the infidels, and move toward 100% Muslim, such as has been experienced and is on-going in:

Bangladesh -- Muslim 83%   Egypt -- Muslim 90%
Gaza -- Muslim 98.7%   Indonesia -- Muslim 86.1%
Iran -- Muslim 98%   Iraq -- Muslim 97%
Jordan -- Muslim 92%   Morocco -- Muslim 98.7%
Pakistan -- Muslim 97%   "Palestine" -- Muslim 99%
Syria -- Muslim 90%   Tajikistan -- Muslim 90%
Turkey -- Muslim 99.8%   United Arab Emirates -- Muslim 96%

100% will usher in the peace of 'Dar-es-Salaam' -- the Islamic House of Peace. Here there's supposed to be peace, because everybody is a Muslim, the Madrasses are the only schools, and the Qur'an is the only word, such as in:

Afghanistan -- Muslim 100%   Saudi Arabia -- Muslim 100%

Somalia -- Muslim 100%   Yemen -- Muslim 100%

In every country where Muslims are in the minority, they are obsessed with minority rights.

In every country with a Muslim majority, there are NO minority rights.

Unfortunately, peace is never achieved, as in these 100% states the most radical Muslims intimidate and spew hatred, and satisfy their blood lust by killing less radical Muslims, for a variety of reasons. In these 100% nations, Muslims seem to be unable to achieve happiness. They're not happy in Gaza. They're not happy in Egypt. They're not happy in Libya, Morocco, Iran, Iraq, Yemen, Afghanistan, Pakistan, Syria or in Lebanon.

So, where are they happy? They're happy in Canada. They're happy in Australia. They're happy in Italy, Germany, Sweden, Denmark, Norway and in the USA. They're happy in every country that is not Muslim. And who do they blame? Not Islam. Not their leadership. Not themselves. They blame the countries they are happy in, and they want to change them to be like the countries they came from where they were unhappy.

"Before I was nine, I had learned the basic canon of Arab life. It was me against my brother; me and my brother against our father; my family against my cousins and the clan; the clan against the tribe; the tribe against the world, and all of us against the infidel." Leon Uris, 'The Haj'

138

In countries such as France, the minority Muslim populations live in ghettos which are 100% Muslim, and within which they live by Sharia Law. The national police do not even enter these ghettos. There are no national courts, nor schools, nor non-Muslim religious facilities. In such enclaves Muslims do not integrate into the community at large. The children attend *madrasses*. They learn only the Qur'an. To even associate with an infidel is a crime punishable with death. And in some areas, Muslim Imams and extremists exercise more power than the national government.

Today's 1.5 billion Muslims make up 22% of the world's population; and their birth rates are higher than those of Christians, Hindus, Buddhists, and Jews. Muslims will exceed 50% of the world's population by the end of this century.

The world is about to change forever.

"Islam is a predatory ideology that oppresses everybody except for the tiny aristocracy at the top. The oppression against Muslim women, half the population, is already infamous. Now you have a good window into the future of the West, if present trends continue." Francisco Gil-White

"One of the great problems with Americans is that –

being a decent people –

they assume that everyone else is equally decent."

RABBI MEIR KAHANE

(Copyright: Jewish Press, New York)

RECOMMENDED READING

Why Be Jewish by Rabbi Meir Kahane - Stein and Day Publishers 1977

Perfidy By Ben Hecht - Milah Press 1997

Uncomfortable Questions for Comfortable Jews by Rabbi Meir Kahane - Lyle Stuart Inc. 1987

The Jewish State, The struggle for Israel's Soul by Yoram Hazony - Basic Books 2000

They Must Go by Rabbi Meir Kahane - The Jewish Idea 1981

Rabbi Meir Kahane, His Life and Thoughts Vol.1 & 2 by Libby Kahane - Urim Pubns, 2008

The Quest for Justice in the Middle East by Gerald Honigman - Strang's Creation House, 2009

The Answer, Does Religion Really Matter? (2nd Edition) by Ze'ev Shemer CreateSpace, 2013

ACKNOWLEDGMENTS

This book was written to honor the memory of my parents, Jeana (Nusha) Sheindl bat Levi z"tl and Zeleman ben Meir z"tl. Their teachings and way of life serve as a role model to our entire family.

To honor the memory of Rabbi Meir Kahane z"tl and his son Rabbi Binyamin Ze'ev Kahane z"tl who were murdered while in the pursuit of justice and the fulfillment of God's commandments; they will forever be a light onto us and to all who dare awaken from the slumber of exile.

I am grateful to my wife Adriana and to my children for putting up with me while I dove for endless hours into this work. They are my inspiration.

I wish to specially thank my sister Silvia, her husband Abraham and their beautiful children. It is the warmth of their home that helped me realize how special Judaism is.

To all who devote much of their lives for the sake of Israel I am thankful. For their contributions and inspiration that added to my own spiritual growth and thus to this work, I would like to express my gratitude to my dear friends and colleagues, Barry Lynn, Shifra Hoffman, Gerald Honigman, Phyllis Chessler, Yoram Ettinger, Steven Shamrak, Emanuel Winston, Jack Golberg, Shmuel HaLevi, Aryeh Zelasko, Shmuel Schachter, Scott Rockwerk, Mike Guzofsky, Lenny

Goldberg, David Halvri, Aryeh Eldad, Aaron Schwarzbaum, Michael Ben Ari, David Wilder; the folks at PMW (Palestinian Media Watch), CAMERA, Israel National News, Outreach Judaism, Aish HaTorah, and Chabad. May HaShem reward you for your Mesirut Nefesh -self sacrifice.

I would also like to express my gratitude and admiration to the amazing Jews of Judea, Samaria, Jerusalem and the Golan Heights who face adversity in their daily lives but show no lessened vitality. To all the people who love and support our state and nation, to our Christian friends, to our Muslim friends, and to all who understand the reasons why this book had to be written.

Thank you.

None of the people mentioned above had any idea that this book would turn out so 'politically incorrect'; but there are many searching souls that will only respond to a direct dosage of truth. I hope not to have done a disservice to the brilliant minds that inspired me to create this work.

RESOURCES

The Disputation; Scholarly Publications, 1972 Jim Kouri, June 2009.

Islamic Terrorism: A brief history lesson for President Barack Obama; Canada Free Press

The Holy Bible: containing the Old and New Testaments in the King James Version; Thomas Nelson Publishers 2009 (Original from Oxford University)

ArtScroll Tanach; (Traditional commentary on the books of the Bible). Mesorah Publications, 1985

The Chumash: The Stone Edition; (Artscroll Series) Mesorah Publications, Limited (June 1993)

The Holy Qur'an; (English translation of the meanings and commentary) The Presidency of Islamic Researches, IFTA, 1989

Genesis and the Big Bang: The Discovery of Harmony between Modern Science and the Bible; Dr. Gerald Shroeder, 1991.. Bantam Publishers 1991

Rabbi Meir Kahane: his life and thought; Libby Kahane, 2009.. Institute for the Publication of the Writings of Rabbi Meir Kahane, 2008

Why Be Jewish; Rabbi Meir Kahane, 1977.. Stein and Day Publishers

Perfidy; Ben Hecht, 1997.. Milah Press

Uncomfortable Questions for Comfortable Jews; Rabbi Meir Kahane, 1987.. Lyle Stuart Inc.

The Jewish State, The struggle for Israel's Soul; Yoram Hazony, 2000.. Basic Books.

They Must Go; Rabbi Meir Kahane, 1981.. The Jewish Idea

BellaOnline's Judaism; Lisa Pinkus, Mideast Outpost, 2004.

Boycott Israel? Do It Properly; by Ed Weiss.

Beheadings and Honor Killings; Phyllis Chesler, 2009. Pajamas Media.

Front Page Magazine.

The Dhimmi: Jews & Christians under Islam; Bat Ye'or and David Maisel, 1985. Fairleigh Dickinson University Press.

Concerning the Jews; Mark Twain, 1899.. Harper's Magazine.

The Conquest of Acre Fortress; Hadar Publishing House Ltd.

Slavery, Terrorism & Islam: The Historical Roots and Contemporary Threat; Peter Hammond, 2005. Christian Liberty Books.

Listen World Listen Jew; Rabbi Meir Kahane, 2005.. Institute for Publication of the Writings of Rabbi Meir Kahane; third edition.

Israel's Ministry of Education (http://www.education.gov.il)

Jewish Agency for Israel

Myths and Facts (Eli Hertz)

Palestinian Media Watch (http://www.palwatch.org/)

Aish HaTorah (http://www.aish.com)

Chabad Lubavitch (http://www.chabad.org)

Stand With Us (http://www.standwithus.com)

Yeshivat Hara'ayon HaYehudi, Jerusalem, Israel.

"Let us not fear the world.
Far better a Jewish State that survives and is hated by the world,
than an Auschwitz that brings us its love and sympathy"
RABBI MEIR KAHANE

DISCLAIMER

The views and opinions expressed in this book are those of the author and do not necessarily reflect the official policy or position of any government or government agency. Examples of policies or historical references within these articles are based only on inferences and assumptions; and the ideas hereby presented are strictly theoretical. In the end, it is up to each of us to choose what to believe in.

www.ingramcontent.com/pod-product-compliance
Lightning Source LLC
Chambersburg PA
CBHW071354310526
45790CB00017B/380